Glastonbury
Origins of the Sacred

Fig. 1.   Glastonbury Abbey, west doorway. Before the Dissolution in 1539 this doorway was blocked by the Lady Chapel's altar. The ancient 'miraculous' image of St Mary, supposedly carved by St Joseph of Arimathea, stood in this area.

Glastonbury

Origins of the Sacred

T.F. Hopkinson-Ball

Antioch Papers
Bristol 2012

First published in 2012 by
Antioch Press, an imprint
of Imagier Publishing
Bristol BS35 3SY
United Kingdom
Email: ip@imagier.com
www.imagier.com

ISBN 13: 978-0-9568789-9-1

Cover and text design by Allan Armstrong
The paper used in this publication is from a
sustainable source and is elemental chlorine free.
Printed and bound by CPI Group (UK) Ltd, Croydon, CR0 4YY

Contents

Illustrations v

Acknowledgements vi

Introduction 1

Ch. 1   The Earliest Evidence 9

Ch. 2   Norman Reticence 13

Ch. 3   The Great Fire and its Consequences 23

Ch. 4   The Bishops of Bath & Glastonbury 33

Ch. 5   The House of the Virgin 45

Ch. 6   St Joseph of Glastonbury 56

Ch. 7   The Final Flowering 67

Epilogue 76

Notes 83

Bibliography 92

Map and Key 97

Index 102

Illustrations

Fig. 1 Glastonbury Abbey, west doorway . . . . (Frontis)

Fig. 2 Glastonbury Abbey interior (reconstructed) . . (opposite page) 1

Fig. 3 Thirteenth century abbey seal 12

Fig. 4 Interior of the Lady Chapel (*c.* 1900) 19

Fig. 5 King Arthur's lead cross 29

Fig. 6 Late medieval arms of Glastonbury Abbey 31

Fig. 7 Statue of St Mary . . . . ' 46

Fig. 8 Arms of St Joseph of Arimathea 57

Fig. 9 Brass Plate from St David's Pillar 61

Fig. 10 St Joseph of Arimathea (stained-glass window) 65

Fig. 11 The IESVS: MARIA stone 79

Fig. 12 Glastonbury Abbey – general plan 98

Fig. 13 Lady Chapel Complex – detailed plan 100

Acknowledgements

Inevitably, I have accumulated numerous debts of gratitude during the writing of this book. I owe particular thanks to Allan Armstrong who dedicated much time and energy to technical problems, Carla Hopkinson-Ball who patiently scrutinised earlier drafts of the text, Tracey Bolt who frequently stimulated my thinking in conversation, Bridget McDermott who supplied boundless reserves of enthusiastic interest, Michael Protheroe who offered numerous constructive comments and Adrian Hopper who has been a listening ear on more than one occasion.

Glastonbury
Michaelmas, 2012

Fig. 2. Glastonbury Abbey, *circa* 1507.
The interior of the great church viewed from the north transept. Imaginative
reconstruction by Frederick Bligh Bond, drawn in 1907.

Introduction

For more than five hundred years the word 'Glastonbury' meant an abbey, not a town. One of the greatest and most ancient in the kingdom, Glastonbury Abbey claimed to be 'the fount and origin of all religion [in England]'.[1] Its abbey church housed the shrines of saints, the tombs of kings, and was the reputed burial place of 'bishops, dukes, abbots and other magnates' so numerous that the chronicler John of Glastonbury passed over their names for 'fear of tedium'.[2] Its mitred abbot sat in the House of Lords, wielded considerable temporal power and was the confidante of kings. In short, Glastonbury was not simply one monastery or pilgrimage destination amongst many; it was, rather, a spiritual powerhouse and a place of wonder. As Henry VIII's commissioners reported to their master, Thomas Cromwell, in the summer of 1539: 'We assure your lordship it is the goodliest house of that sort that ever we have seen. We would that your lordship did know it as we do; then we doubt not but your lordship would judge it a house meet for the king's majesty, and for no man else.'[3]

As one of only a handful of English religious houses commonly regarded as 'great and solemn' monasteries, the 'convent of St Mary of Glaston' boasted a rich and varied cultural life. Set behind an embattled precinct wall, embellished with 'many rich and stately pictures cut in stone',[4] were some

1

60 acres over which sprawled an impressive array of buildings.[5] By the Dissolution, the monastery reflected nearly 350 years of uninterrupted architectural development and almost unlimited spending power. Its great church surpassed the cathedral in Wells, its treasury contained 'antiquities and wonders', and its books and charters were housed in one of medieval England's largest libraries. Its vast estates and economic power resulted in earthly grandeur, but at the heart of all this was the *Opus Dei* (the work of God) - the daily rhythm of worship consisting of the Daily Offices and Masses. But why was Glastonbury so renowned? The medieval answer to this question, the *raison d'être* which explained the abbey's very existence, was its foundation legend - the story of Glastonbury's sacred origins.

The purpose of this publication is to provide a brief yet accessible overview of the first five hundred years of story-telling about Glastonbury's beginnings, tracing the cumulative effect of its telling and retelling over the centuries, and offering a few general observations along the way. For convenience sake I have presented this study in seven chapters, although the text constitutes one continuous narrative and concludes with a short epilogue. Despite the subject matter being quite complex, this is not an academic study and so I have kept endnotes to a minimum. We will not, however, be addressing the literal truth of Glastonbury's foundation story. If you are searching for an historical exploration of the reality of King Arthur's or St Joseph of Arimathea's role in Glastonbury's past you will not find it within these pages, nor is this a general history of Glastonbury Abbey. Rather, we will be addressing the story itself, what was thought and believed to be true in the Middle

Introduction

Ages, and how this narrative was built upon from generation to generation, before the dissolution of the monasteries forced the abbey's closure in 1539.

In this respect, the archaeology of the abbey precinct is a largely peripheral matter which seems not to have impinged significantly upon our story. However, we should observe that the archaeology of Glastonbury Abbey strongly supports its ancient origins. Enough evidence survives to suggest that the abbey stands on or adjacent to the site of a high-status Roman building, almost certainly a villa, probably built by a local Romanised British family. Although this might come as a surprise to some who prefer the notion of an early Christian community established on a virgin site, we know historically speaking that there is nothing very remarkable about a monastery rising in a previously occupied location. In some parts of the Latin west, villas evolved into faith communities and then later into what we now think of as monasteries. In Somerset and Wiltshire there are numerous late Roman sites with evidence of Christian use, such as the fifth-century baptistery in the Roman villa at Bradford upon Avon, while at Wells, just seven miles from Glastonbury, the ancient nucleus of the cathedral was seemingly a Roman or sub-Roman mausoleum. At Glastonbury, an unbroken pottery sequence has been recovered through excavation, stretching from the late Iron Age, through the Roman, sub-Roman and into the Saxon, including high-status wares in every period. This implies not only continued occupation of the abbey site in Glastonbury, but the presence of high-status pottery, especially in the sub-Roman period, also suggests something out of the ordinary was happening. Combined with the earliest and most substantial archaeological evidence for glass-making in Saxon Britain dating approximately to the 680s, probably associated with a major rebuilding of the abbey undertaken by King Ine of Wessex, the archaeology suggests that while Glastonbury's medieval monks may not have known when or by whom their abbey had been founded, they were right to claim that it had ancient and exceptional origins.

But although archaeology supports the claim that Glastonbury Abbey genuinely does have early origins, we must sound a note of caution. Continuity of occupation does *not* presuppose continuity of belief. As yet, nothing has been discovered in the abbey precinct which illuminates the religious beliefs or practices of its earliest occupants and it would be unwise for us to speculate about them. All we can say at present is that Glastonbury was important from an early period, but we do not know why. We should also stress that although the abbey eventually claimed a first-century foundation date and founder, this does not imply that the medieval monks understood or were aware of the antiquity of their house, archaeologically speaking. In other words, the foundation story was a pious fiction which owed its creation to happy coincidence rather than inspiration based on the literal relics of Roman Britain.

We will also be exploring the context which contributed to the origin story's growth and highlighting an element frequently overlooked by Glastonbury historians–the role of lived spirituality and material religion. In other words we will look at sacred objects, events, personalities and phenomena in medieval Glastonbury, all of which formed equally important

Introduction

influences on our story's development – either by prompting revisions and contributing new elements, or even causing events on the ground, both literary and literal, which in turn fed back into the foundation story's evolution. Admittedly this is a difficult task, as almost all our evidence for material religion and lived spirituality in medieval Glastonbury is now literary – only descriptions of objects and events survive – but it remains pivotal none the less. It is difficult to underestimate the importance of sacred objects and divine intervention to the medieval mind, and this is something of which we should certainly remind ourselves while exploring the origin story's context.

Although often forgotten today, medieval religious houses either knew precisely when they had been established and who was responsible or, if they were particularly ancient and their origins somewhat hazy, they promulgated foundation stories to establish and explain their origins. As we shall see, the surviving medieval sources addressing Glastonbury's origins demonstrate that foundation stories were not fixed; rather, they slowly grew in elaboration, developing as the centuries passed. Even a cursory glance at these stories suggests that medieval culture was not rigidly proscribed by a monolithic Catholic church but was hospitable to the extraordinary. In this regard, although the story which explained Glastonbury's origins may appear fabulous to us it was not exceptional. The monastic community of Westminster, for example, maintained that its house had been founded on the site of a Roman temple of Apollo in the second century by the mythical British Christian King Lucius and that in the seventh century St Peter himself had miraculously consecrated their abbey church.

Glastonbury: Origins of the Sacred

Through the story of its foundation, a church explained its existence and proclaimed its sanctity, both to itself and to the wider world. But these were no simple tales; the range of allusion they contain is often dense and not easily digested, and these stories should not necessarily be taken at face value. Combined with the fact that we are considering texts in translation and that translations can vary markedly, we must proceed carefully in our quest. While we may tease apart original texts from later additions or attempt to date early charters to their actual time of composition, it is highly unlikely that the medieval reader or author would have understood our concerns or even cared about them if they did. A 'forged' medieval charter or text was not forged in the modern sense of the word; rather it recorded in writing what was known to be true, believed to be true or even *ought* to have been true about a place, person or event. We should also ask ourselves whether an author understood the difference between history and legend? Was an author's motivation pious or political? Who was the audience for which an author's work was intended? Our concerns and priorities today are not necessarily those of our ancestors and it is important not to confuse our preoccupations with theirs.

We must also be mindful that written materials become dated. It is all too easy to assume that the manuscripts and charters in a medieval library were constantly in use, whereas they aged and became unfashionable as books do today. Just because William of Malmesbury referred to a manuscript in the 1120s for example, does not necessarily mean that it was still available a century later. As a privilege in Glastonbury's 'Great Chartulary' (a fourteenth-century collection of abbey deeds and charters)

Introduction

observes, sometimes there are no documents to be seen, 'since some have perished of age, others have been burned and others lost by hostile acts or other accidents'.[6] Manuscripts were also updated, revised, improved and edited for a variety of different reasons and it is often difficult or indeed impossible accurately to trace these changes in surviving works. We must also remind ourselves that literary materials were not freely available for the scrutiny of all, even those who could read. Indeed, throughout the Middle Ages, libraries and archives were exclusive domains to which only the privileged were admitted – and even then sparingly. When the historian John Leland required access to Glastonbury's library in the 1530s, wisely he brought a letter of introduction from the king himself to guarantee sight of the abbey's collection.

Over the last century, Glastonbury's history and traditions have received considerable academic attention. During this time the abbey's foundation legend has been addressed in texts by scholars from a variety of different backgrounds, many of which are utilised in this work. But despite such industry, we must not forget that our assessment of Glastonbury's past stands solely on the literary and physical remains of a medieval abbey; only forty or so manuscripts come down to us from a library which may have held thousands of volumes and perhaps 5 per cent of the monastic buildings survive to the present day. As we shall discover, notwithstanding such losses and the passing of nearly half a millennium, although the principal elements of Glastonbury's foundation story are known and relatively straight-forward, it none the less constitutes a surprisingly complex tale. In consequence, there is much we will only briefly touch upon and far more which we must, of necessity, leave out. Bearing all this in mind, we shall now turn to the story of Glastonbury's sacred origins and through its exploration we might come to understand why medieval Glastonbury came to be dubbed England's 'holyest erth',[7] and reflect upon the largely forgotten story which still underlies Glastonbury's attraction for so many people today.

Chapter 1: The Earliest Evidence

Glastonbury's early history is represented by its charters.[8] However, as the historian Lesley Abrams has observed, 'there are many interesting points on which they fail to inform us. The difficult question of Glastonbury's origins is first on this list of silences.'[9] When we consider that this charter evidence is also 'fragmentary, incomplete, and mostly put together many years after the period to which it applied'[10] we might despair, but fortunately for us they contain little of relevance to the *story* of the abbey's sacred origins and so we have no need to consider them in detail, other than making a few general observations. The earliest charter widely accepted as authentic, albeit only extant in a tenth-century copy, is a land grant dated 681. This was given by the West Saxon sub-king Baldred to the 'church of blessed Mary and blessed Patrick' at Glastonbury, although the annexation of St Patrick to the dedication may be a later addition.[11] A charter of King Ine of Wessex, witnessed by St Aldhelm just over twenty years later in 704, described this church as the 'wooden church' (*lignea basilica*), while an addition to the *Anglo-Saxon Chronicle* records that Ine built the first stone minster church at Glastonbury which was dedicated to SS Peter and Paul. In the centuries that followed, the wooden church started to be called the 'Ealdechirche' or 'Old Church' (*Vetusta Ecclesia*); more formally it was known as the Church of St Mary.[12]

Glastonbury: Origins of the Sacred

Having established that by the late seventh century there was seemingly a church dedicated to the Virgin in Glastonbury, we can turn to the earliest surviving written account of Glastonbury's sacred origins. This is to be found in the first *Vita Dunstanae* (Life of St Dunstan).[13] Written *circa* 1000, we only know the *Vita*'s author by the initial 'B', but it seems likely that he knew St Dunstan personally. As Dunstan had spent his early years living near Glastonbury and was educated at the abbey, it is probable that 'B' recorded local traditions that were current at the time. The relevant passage regarding the origins of the church of Glastonbury appears close to the beginning of the *Vita*. Having introduced Heorstan and Cynethryth, Dunstan's father and mother, 'B' continues, describing the Glastonbury of his day:

> Now in Heorstan's neighbourhood there was an island belonging to the crown, the Old English name for which was Glastonbury. It spread wide its curving shores, surrounded as it was by waters in which fish abounded and by river swamps. It was well suited to the many requirements of human need, and, what is most important, it was given over to the holy service of God.[14]

The locality of this royal island having been established in general terms, 'B' addresses its church's origins. As the Latin of the original is open to slight but significant variance in translation, the following two passages are offered for comparative purposes. The first is from the latest academic translation of the *Vita*, while the second is a more flamboyant translation, redolent of the Englished versions of the *Vita* produced in the nineteenth and twentieth centuries:

> For it was in this island that, by God's guidance, the first novices of the catholic law discovered an ancient church, not built or dedicated in the memory of man. Later, the builder of the heavens Himself revealed by many miraculous and supernatural happenings that it was consecrated to Him and His holy Mother Mary. To this church they added a second, building it of stone and the bishops dedicated it to Christ and his apostle St Peter.[15]

Or alternatively:

> For it was indeed in that very place that the first neophytes of the Catholic law were directed of old by God to rediscover a church, not built by men's skill, but rather prepared in heaven for the salvation of mankind; afterwards the Maker of the heavens Himself demonstrated by many miraculous deeds and mysteries that this church was consecrated to His Mother [or, in a second MS, the Mother of God] Mary. Here also they came to add an oratory built of stone, which at the behest of Christ Himself they dedicated to St Peter the Apostle.[16]

Whichever of these translations better catches the spirit of the Latin original is in a sense unimportant; as Geoffrey Ashe observed back in 1957: 'The fable of the miraculous founding is evidence of two things – first, antiquity: and second, oblivion.'[17] In other words, while it was well known that Glastonbury was ancient, nobody knew how this holy house of prayer had been established or who was responsible, and it was this fact which opened the door to the foundation story's development. But this is to anticipate. We should observe however, that the 'novices' or 'neophytes of the Catholic law' of whom 'B' writes, presumably represent first or second-generation Anglo-Saxon Christian converts and that they discovered a structure which was interpreted as an ancient church. We should also note that despite the lack of a named founder or precise date when this church was established, it is clear that Glastonbury was regarded as a special place, chosen by Christ and dedicated to His mother. This dedication to St Mary, whether genuinely ancient or a relatively recent (i.e. Anglo-Saxon) innovation as some scholars have suggested would increase in importance as the centuries progressed.

Fig. 3. Thirteenth-century abbey seal. (see front cover) The legend reads: SIGILLVM SANCTE MARIA GLASTONIE (Seal of [the Church of] St Mary of Glastonbury). It seems likely that the central figure is a stylised depiction of the 'miraculous' image of Our Lady of Glastonbury.

Chapter 2: Norman Reticence

After William, Duke of Normandy's conquest of England in 1066, Glastonbury's last Saxon abbot was deposed and in the decades which followed a succession of Norman ecclesiastics ruled the abbey. Despite being the wealthiest monastery in the kingdom and the burial place of kings Edmund the Elder, Edgar and Edmund Ironside, this period of transition was a difficult one for the largely Saxon community as the new hierarchy had little respect for English customs.[18] The old abbey church of SS Peter and Paul was gradually demolished and a grand new Romanesque building rose in its place. Unusually, if not uniquely, the ancient Church of St Mary was left untouched despite its humble and no doubt dilapidated appearance. Even Henry of Blois (1126-1171), Glastonbury's greatest Norman abbot and a man known for his energetic building schemes, respected the Old Church's integrity: seemingly it was deemed too sacred to be rebuilt. Indeed, through Abbot Blois' inspiration, not only were the major feasts of the Virgin Mary celebrated with greater zeal and devotion, but the abbot also paid for a candle to burn perpetually before the statue of St Mary which stood in the Old Church.

But despite such reverence for the abbey's heavenly patron and its noble past, a detailed foundation story was still lacking, as were the relics of particularly famous saints — at least in

Norman eyes. Throughout the Middle Ages a monastery's sanctity and piety revealed itself in its collection of holy relics. It was believed that the possession of relics was in itself an indicator of spiritual worth, for the bodily remains of the saints would not remain with the spiritually unworthy. In this regard Glastonbury had been particularly well served over the centuries. A renowned burial place of the blessed, august donors such as King Edgar had also presented the abbey with many significant relics, such as the head of St Apollinaris the martyr and bones belonging to St Vincent of Saragossa. But despite such treasures many native British saints were regarded with suspicion by the new Norman hierarchy and they were not initially accorded the honours which they had once been granted. Worse than this, Glastonbury's greatest son, St Dunstan, who as Archbishop of Canterbury had overseen a root and branch reform of the English Church in the tenth century, was enshrined in his cathedral church in far away Kent. Gradually, as Glastonbury's Saxon and Norman communities merged and attitudes to native saints softened under the guidance of Archbishop Anselm at Canterbury, the situation improved, but it was accepted at Glastonbury that something needed to be done to reassert the abbey's prominence. The issue became pressing after a *Life* of St Dunstan composed at Canterbury claimed that the saint was Glastonbury's first abbot, which, of course, implied that the abbey was of no great age or significance.

And so, in an attempt to demonstrate their monastery's spiritual standing to the wider world, its community turned to an outsider to record and amplify their history. The man they commissioned was an Anglo-Norman whom we know today as William of Malmesbury. The foremost historian of the twelfth century, William was a Benedictine monk from Malmesbury Abbey in Wiltshire where in about 1125 he wrote one of the most important historical works of the European Middle Ages, the *Gesta Regum Anglorum* (The Deeds of the English Kings).[19] It was just a few years later, *circa* 1129, that he compiled the *De Antiquitate Glastonie Ecclesie* (On the Antiquities of the Church of Glastonbury). Having already composed a number of saints' lives for the abbey, William seemingly had free access to Glastonbury's library and archives when compiling his chronicle.[20] Unfortunately for us however, the earliest surviving copy of the *De Antiquitate* is a heavily revised version produced *circa* 1247, some one hundred and twenty years after the composition of the original. This mid-thirteenth-century manuscript version contains numerous later additions and it is difficult to disentangle William's original work from later layers of accretion. Problematic though this is, for the most part we can tell what William actually wrote in his original manuscript of *De Antiquitate*, as he inserted extracts from it in his third revision of the *Gesta Regum*, and it is to these texts to which we first turn.

William offers us not one, but *two* versions of Glastonbury's origins. Firstly, the reader is presented with an account of Britain's conversion in which William follows the Venerable Bede.[21] Like his illustrious predecessor, William refers to the tradition, first found in the *Liber Pontificalis* (The Book of the Pontiffs)[22] begun *circa* 530, that Pope Eleutherius sent preachers to Britain in the late second century:

> We are told by trustworthy annals that Lucius king of the British sent Eleutherius, thirteenth successor of St. Peter, to beg that he would lighten

the darkness of Britain with the rays of Christian preaching. O brave king, and worthy of all praise his undertaking! That faith which in those days nearly all kings and people persecuted when it was presented to them, he went out of his way to ask for when he had scarce heard of it. So preachers sent by Eleutherius came to Britain, where their work shall endure forever, although many years' oblivion has devoured their names. The ancient church of St Mary at Glastonbury was their handiwork, as the faithful tradition of succeeding centuries recounts.[23]

No longer of uncertain origin, Glastonbury's ancient church of St Mary is now claimed to have been built by Pope Eleutherius' second-century emissaries, rather than discovered by 'novices' or 'neophytes of the catholic law'. This story also established two clear links, firstly between Glastonbury and Rome and, secondly, between Glastonbury and the monarchy, specifically its role in establishing Christianity in Britain. Following this passage, William presents us with a shortened version of the original story which 'B' told in his *Vita* of St Dunstan:

There is too that trustworthy record found in several sources, which declares that no other hands made the church of Glastonbury, but it was Christ's disciples themselves that built it. Nor is this unlikely; for if the Apostle Philip preached to the Gauls, as Freculf says in Book 2, Chapter 4, we can well believe that he also sowed the seed of his preaching across the sea. But I would not be thought to deceive my readers' expectations with romantic fancies; and therefore, leaving these points of difference undecided, I will set to and tell a story of solid truth.[24]

Note that these unnamed 'neophytes of the catholic law' in William's version of 'B's text have now been transformed into Christ's disciples, not just early or first generation Anglo-Saxon converts, but first-century Christians perhaps associated with St Philip the Apostle. Be this as it may, as William's final sentence makes clear, he was somewhat sceptical about this second version of Glastonbury's foundation story, but for completeness' sake he included it in his narrative.

William also makes a further reference to Christ's special relationship with Glastonbury. Towards the end of the sixth century, St David of Wales, accompanied by seven other Welsh bishops, is said to have come to Glastonbury to dedicate its church, as the 'antiquity and holiness of the church was established through him by a heavenly vision'. On the night before the proposed dedication ceremony, St David retired to bed:

> When he was sound asleep, he saw standing beside him the Lord Jesus, who gently asked the reason for his coming. He explained without hesitation; whereupon the Lord turned him from his purpose, saying that He had long since dedicated the church in honour of His Mother, and it was wrong for such a sacrament to be repeated, and so profaned, by the hand of man. At the same moment, in the dream, the Lord pierced with His finger the palm of his

hand, and said: 'Behold a sign that what I have done already must not be repeated. Nevertheless, inasmuch as you were motivated by piety and not by presumption, your penalty shall not last long. In the morning, at Mass, when you come to the "With Him and through Him and in Him", you shall be fully restored to health and strength.' The bishop awoke in terror. He grew pale then at the running sore on his hand, and later no less surely welcomed the truth of the prophecy. And, that his journey might not seem fruitless, he quickly built and dedicated another church.[25]

This story was apparently composed by William as a response to the claim made in the first *Vita Dauidis* (Life of St David) written by the Welsh monk and scholar Rhigyfarch around 1095.[26] In this work Rhigyfarch claimed that Glastonbury, along with the monastery of Bath, were among the churches founded by St David late in his career – which at a stroke made the Somerset monasteries inferior to the saint's Welsh houses.[27] Not surprisingly, it was a story that the Glastonbury monks virulently rejected; William's riposte makes it clear that not only had Glastonbury been founded long before St David's time, but it had been consecrated by Christ Himself in honour of His mother. But although this story made Glastonbury's superiority to the church in Wales abundantly clear, it did not detract from St David's importance to Glastonbury. Indeed, during the abbacy of Henry of Blois a 'great sapphire' was supposedly discovered (probably a porphyry slab used as a portable altar) which according to tradition had been brought to Glastonbury by St David himself and had been

Fig. 4. The interior of the Lady Chapel from the east (*circa* 1900), with the crypt chapel of St Joseph exposed below. The floor which separated the two chapels collapsed after the Dissolution.

given to the saint by the Patriarch of Jerusalem. Hidden away in a recess of a door in St Mary's Church, Abbot Blois had the 'great sapphire' removed and adorned with gold, silver and precious stones. It remained as an object of veneration for the rest of the monastery's history.[28]

Turning now to the revised version of the *De Antiquitate* and those portions of the text we can with a reasonable degree of certainty attribute to William, the eighteenth chapter addresses 'the sanctity and dignity of the church of Glastonbury'. First stating that it 'is the oldest of all those that I know of in England and hence the epithet applied to it [i.e. the Old Church]', William goes on to highlight the abbey's collection of holy relics:

> In it are preserved the bodily remains of many saints, besides Patrick and the others of whom I spoke above, and there is no part of the church that is without the ashes of the blessed. The stone-paved floor, the sides of the altar itself, above and within, are filled with relics close-packed. Deservedly indeed is the repository of so many saints said to be a heavenly shrine on earth. How fortunate, good Lord, are those inhabitants who have been summoned to an upright life by reverence for that place. I cannot believe that any of these can fail of heaven, for their deaths are accompanied by the recommendation and advocacy of such great patrons. There one can observe all over the floor stones, artfully interlaced in the forms of triangles or squares and sealed with lead; I do no harm to religion if I believe some sacred mystery is contained beneath them.[29]

Norman Reticence

Central to this passage is the doctrine of the Communion of Saints. This, Christians believe, is the spiritual solidarity which binds together the faithful on earth, the souls in purgatory and the saints in heaven in the unity of the same mystical body under Christ. William is suggesting that this link is particularly strong at Glastonbury because of the presence in the Old Church of the relics of the abbey's 'great patrons'. Saints such as Patrick, Indract and Gildas stand as intercessors at the heavenly court for all who come to pray devotedly at the abbey. William's final somewhat cryptic reference to the chapel's floor continues to be a source of speculation. Whether he was referring to a modern (in William's terms) mosaic or tiled floor, or perhaps something older is impossible to tell at this remove; likewise, what he meant us to understand by the 'sacred mystery' sealed 'beneath' or perhaps embodied in the floor's design, is unclear. However, the historian Antonia Gransden has offered an alternative translation of the final enigmatic sentence which better fits the passage which precedes it: 'I do no injustice to religion if I believe that wherever a stone triangle or square is deliberately placed in the paving, carefully set and bonded in lead, there lies some hidden holy relic.'[30] We should also observe that earlier in the same passage William informs us that the 'stone-paved floor' is 'filled with relics close packed'; the pavement thus becomes symbolic of the saints both supporting the faithful as they pray in the Old Church and constituting the building blocks of the church universal. But the pavement's importance lies not only in its meaning, but in its function. Acting as a carpet of honour before the altar, over which a priest would walk and stand at the celebration of the mass, it was a rare and expensive luxury in the twelfth century. Whether it concealed some obscure esoteric meaning or the relics of saints, or both, it clearly signalled the Old Church's sanctity and high status.

Although modern scholars praise William of Malmesbury for being a cautious and accurate historian, Glastonbury's monks do not seem to have been particularly impressed by his rather conservative approach and William's chronicle was soon thought to be dated. To quote John Scott, the most recent editor of the *De Antiquitate*:

> Yet for all William's skill and his success in establishing the antiquity of Glastonbury and the aura of sanctity that had always pervaded it the monks soon found that it was no longer adequate for their needs. They found themselves in a new world, facing different challenges that could not be parried by boasting of the great age of their monastery or celebrating the glorious Celtic saints who had made pilgrimages to it.[31]

In consequence, William's chronicle would be continually 'improved' and Glastonbury was soon to suffer a disaster which would stimulate such textual 'improvements' on an unprecedented scale.

Chapter 3: The Great Fire and its Consequences

Barely fifty years after William of Malmesbury had completed his chronicle, Glastonbury Abbey suffered its only major disaster, the Great Fire of 1184. Devastating the entire monastery, it left a single chamber with its chapel and a bell tower undamaged. It is not known how or where the fire started, but its consequences would be far-reaching. Fortunately for the monks, King Henry II came to their aid and with royal patronage the beginning of reconstruction was swift.

The king's official at Glastonbury, his chamberlain Ralph Fitzstephen, 'finished St Mary's Church on the spot where the Old Church had originally stood, using squared stones and the most attractive workmanship, and he spared nothing in its ornamentation'.[32] This new Church of St Mary which also doubled as the Lady Chapel, is the roofless building which still stands at the west end of the abbey ruins today. Consecrated by Reginald, Bishop of Bath, just two years after the fire, the new chapel was built in a deliberately old-fashioned style to echo the antiquity of the Old Church it replaced. The interior of the new Church of St Mary was extravagantly painted with rare and costly pigments, and lit with richly coloured glass; pilgrims would have been in no doubt that they were on holy ground.

Unsurprisingly, the fire prompted a profound shift in the abbey's spiritual geography and inevitably this impacted on the story of Glastonbury's origins. Before 1184 the Old Church had been the abbey's ancient sacred centre, while the Norman abbey church to the east with its tombs and memorials had been a clear visual statement of the monastery's dignity and power. Such buildings were an indisputable proof of age, literally demonstrating the length and quality of a monastery's pedigree. But in the fire, all this was lost. The oldest church in the land supposedly built by the first British Christians had perished. A new focus had to be found as the story of Glastonbury's ancient origins could no longer be taken for granted. Now they had to be clearly emphasised. After all, for many years after 1184, a pilgrim arriving at the abbey would have found a building site where almost everything was new.

It is little surprise then that an ancient wooden statue of the Virgin, the only object from the Old Church which survived the fire intact, suddenly took on a profound new significance. According to a passage later inserted in William of Malmesbury's *De Antiquitate*, this statue:

> was not touched – not even the veil that hung from its head – by the great fire that surrounded the altar and consumed the cloth and all the ornaments on it. Yet because of the fire's heat blisters, like those on a living man, arose on its face and remained visible for a long time to all who looked, testifying to a divine miracle.[33]

The Great Fire and its Consequences

The chronicler John of Glastonbury (see below) later repeated this story, but added the following comment, noting that the blisters were 'a worthy demonstration of the miracle that fire could not touch the image of her who remained ever virgin in body and mind and who knew no lust of the flesh. Thus the holy Mother of God herself defended her image from fire and showed that she is able, with the greatest ease, to free those who serve her from the fire of hell.'[34] This ancient statue thus became a tangible link and perhaps the only direct visual link, in the new Church of St Mary (the Lady Chapel) to Glastonbury's lost past. Granting a direct sense of continuity between the two buildings, the statue and its miraculous survival stood as incontrovertible proof that Glastonbury's patron, St Mary the Virgin, watched over the community and regarded it as her own. The statue and all that it symbolised would inevitably affect the evolving story of Glastonbury's sacred origins.

The most important example of the Virgin's growing ascendancy is contained in the *Carta Henrici regis secundi* ('Great Privilege' or Charter of King Henry II). The earliest surviving copy of this document is contained in the work of another of the abbey's monkish chroniclers, Adam of Domerham.[35] According to the privilege, it was issued at Westminster shortly after the great fire of 1184 and it confirmed all Glastonbury's ancient liberties and dignities which had been granted by King Henry's royal predecessors.

The authenticity of the *Carta Henrici* as it comes down to us has been doubted, especially as some of the witnesses who supposedly signed it were dead at the time of its writing. The signatories do however include Heraclius, Latin Patriarch of Jerusalem, who was in London in the autumn of 1184 to consecrate the Temple Church. This perhaps indicates that the charter is authentic and was originally written shortly after the Great Fire and signed by those present in London at the time, although later embellished with other names to give it greater standing. Its importance for us, none the less, lies not so much in its literal authenticity as a legal document, but in the statement it contains regarding Glastonbury's origin and status. Here is the appropriate passage:

> whatever has been confirmed in these documents to the aforesaid church - which was once called by some the Mother of Saints, by others the Tomb of Saints, and which the venerable authority of the ancients holds to have been built by the Lord's very disciples and first dedicated by the very Lord himself – I also concede, to the honour of God and of the most blessed Virgin Mary, who in this kingdom first chose that place especially for herself, and to the honour of all the saints who rest there.[36]

Whether or not these words were written by the king's scribes, added to the charter by a contemporary Glastonbury monk or inserted retrospectively at the abbey, is in a sense irrelevant. What is important here, is that the Great Fire of 1184 allowed the community to re-imagine their past and build on what had gone before. And it is this charter, supposedly granted by King Henry in the fire's immediate aftermath, which provided a literal royal seal of approval (spurious or not) on Glastonbury's unique position. Firstly, the abbey is provided with two new fittingly grandiose titles, the 'Mother

The Great Fire and its Consequences

of Saints' (*Mater Sanctorum*) and the 'Tomb of Saints' (*Tumulus Sanctorum*). The first epithet, 'Mother of Saints', reflects not just the abbey's role as an educational centre, but also its dedication to the Virgin, while the second title, 'Tomb of Saints', clearly refers to the numerous relics and burials of the blessed the abbey sheltered. It is then stated that not only did the Lord's disciples establish the Old Church and that Christ had personally dedicated it, but for the first time it is claimed that the Virgin had chosen Glastonbury 'especially for herself'. While the exact meaning of this enigmatic statement is left unexplained, it may imply that the 'miraculous' survival of St Mary's statue in the Great Fire was interpreted by the monastic community as a mark of particular favour. Whatever the text's precise meaning, its implication is clear; Glastonbury was established as a shrine of national importance. While other churches laid claim the tombs of great saints such at Thomas at Canterbury, Swithun at Winchester and Cuthbert at Durham, Glastonbury alone claimed to be England's first and premier shrine of the Mother of God.

The 1184 fire not only resulted in the granting (or creation) of charters, but it also stimulated the revision of already existing documents. It seems to have been in the fire's aftermath, for example, that many such additions were made to William of Malmesbury's *De Antiquitate*. One such addition is the book's third chapter, which consists of an anecdote regarding Godfrey, a Glastonbury monk, which allegedly arose during Henry of Blois' time as abbot.[37] According to this anonymous writer, while Godfrey was staying at the abbey of St Denis in Paris, he fell into conversation with one of the older French monks. During

27

Godfrey's conversation with his unnamed French counterpart, he was asked the following question:

> Where do your people come from? Where do you live?' He replied, 'I am a Norman monk, father, from the monastery in Britain that is called Glastonbury.' 'Is that ancient church of the perpetual Virgin and compassionate mother still standing?', he asked. 'It is', the monk said. At this the elder, who was gently stroking Godfrey's head, remained wrapt in silence for a long time and at length spoke thus. 'This church of the most glorious martyr Denis and that which you claim as yours share the same honour and privilege the one in France, the other in Britain; they both arose at the same time and each was consecrated by the highest and greatest priest. Yet in one degree yours is superior, for it is called a second Rome.' While he was hanging on that man's words, the guest-master separated them from each other, despite their reluctance, and they never saw each other again. But no more of this.[38]

The importance of this passage for us lies not just in the bold assertion that the abbeys of Glastonbury and St Denis were of equal dignity – St Denis was the French royal burial church which claimed to have been founded by St Paul's disciple, Dionysius the Areopagite in the first century[39] – but also in the application of the title 'Second Rome' (*Roma Secunda*) to Glastonbury which made it 'superior' to St Denis by 'one degree'. This epithet was clearly not intended as a claim to near equality of precedence with Rome, let alone the pretence of an 'independent' English church as some scholars have suggested.[40] On the contrary, a number of Glastonbury charters show that the abbey placed itself under the pope's jurisdiction and looked to the Holy See for protection.[41] Rather, the title 'Second Rome' – like 'Mother of Saints' and 'Tomb of Saints' - was an accolade given to an ancient, powerful and august monastery to acknowledge, bolster and propagate its growing reputation for sanctity.

It was less than a decade after the Great Fire when perhaps the single most important event in Glastonbury's history occurred, the claimed unearthing of the bodies of King Arthur and Queen Guinevere. Much has been written about the circumstances leading up to the discovery and its later ramifications, none of which we need to consider in any detail.[42] Suffice it to say, during an excavation between two ancient 'pyramids' (tall standing cross-shafts) in the Old Cemetery to the south of the Lady Chapel, a lead cross was found, bearing the inscription: 'Here lies buried the renowned King Arthur in the Isle of Avalon'.[43] At an even greater depth the remains of two bodies were discovered in a wooden coffin. The mortal remains of

Fig. 5. King Arthur's lead cross (after Camden 1695).

Arthur and Guinevere had been found and, although some contemporaries had their doubts, the story seems to have been generally accepted and the discovery quickly became a part of established medieval Arthurian tradition.

The consensus today amongst historians and archaeologists is that the discovery was an elaborate fraud, a deliberate hoax perpetrated by the monks to assist their recovery from the precarious financial position in which the fire had left them. While the excavation undoubtedly attracted national attention, there is no evidence that King Arthur's remains significantly increased pilgrimage traffic or donations to the abbey. The supposed royal bones were *not* instantly transferred to a magnificent new tomb to which 'pilgrims' flocked, quite the contrary. Instead, they were placed close to a chapel in the south transept of the great church. There they were to remain for the next eighty-seven years until in 1278 King Edward I ordered their removal to a more prominent position. At the time of a state visit the royal bones were transferred to a grand and highly decorated black marble sarcophagus. Two stone lions were placed at each end of the tomb, an image of King Arthur on its west face, a crucifix on its east face and the leaden cross found during the excavation was placed above it. When this tomb was erected before the high altar of the abbey church, Arthur and Guinevere's 'heads and cheeks (*sic, 'genis'*) were kept out on account of the devotion of the people.'[44] This veneration of the royal couples' remains as though they were saints' relics demonstrates that even though Arthur and Guinevere were not canonised, they were clearly regarded as holy by monks and laity alike.

In hindsight, the significance of the discovery – fraudulent or not – was enormous. Growing and multiplying in the context of the centuries which followed, it grounded the mythic, British Arthur in the very real English soil of Glastonbury, with all the national and international political point-scoring it would provide for future English kings and their imperial pretentions. But this is all beyond the scope of this study. As to why Arthur

The Great Fire and its Consequences

Fig. 6. Late medieval arms
of Glastonbury Abbey.

had become associated with Glastonbury in the first place, it is enough to observe that most scholars have accepted Caradoc of Llancarvan's *Vita Gildae* (Life of St Gildas) written for the monks of Glastonbury *circa* 1140, as the precipitating factor, as it is the earliest surviving text to associate Glastonbury with King Arthur. But Arthur himself did not significantly impact upon the abbey's foundation narrative, other than reinforcing St Mary's continued importance in the evolving legends. Both Geoffrey of Monmouth and Nennius before him claimed that Arthur fought with an image of the Virgin on his shield, 'which forced him to think perpetually of her'.[45] Thus, when Arthur's Marian credentials were combined with the abbey's, it is perhaps not surprising that it was later claimed that the king had attended a mystical Mass at Beckery just outside Glastonbury, at which not only were both the Christ Child and St Mary present, but after which the Virgin personally presented Arthur with a rock-crystal cross as a memento of the occasion. Indeed, the abbey affirmed that this relic was preserved in its treasury and throughout the Middle Ages the Virgin's cross was regularly carried in procession through the great church on Wednesdays and Fridays in Lent. This secondary relic of the Virgin and its origins were considered so significant by the Glastonbury community that, from at least the beginning of the fifteenth century, both the Virgin and her cross were depicted on the abbey's official shield of arms.[46]

But equally as important to Glastonbury was Arthur's mere presence at the abbey. As James Carley has succinctly observed, 'in c. 1191 King Arthur's body was discovered in the abbey cemetery and as a result Glastonbury became publically identified as Avalon. Glastonbury's whole political future, nationally and internationally, was ultimately determined by this identification, since Joseph came to Glastonbury, as it were, via Avalon.' In other words, it was from the tangled thicket of Arthurian romance, which went hand in hand with Arthur's presence at the abbey, from which St Joseph of Arimathea – the 'noble Decurion'[47] of St Mark's Gospel – was eventually to emerge as Glastonbury's sub-apostolic founder.[48] We must be careful however, not get ahead of ourselves. With the discovery of Arthur's grave, Glastonbury could claim the tomb of Britain's greatest Christian king, but important as Arthur's exhumation undoubtedly was, he was only essential to the abbey's spiritual life and origins by default. While the monastic community was doubtless gratified by the discovery, it would soon have a more pressing and surprisingly modern matter with which to occupy their time – a hostile corporate takeover.

Chapter 4: The Bishops of Bath and Glastonbury

Despite Glastonbury's growing confidence, the years following the fire of 1184 saw the greatest single threat to the abbey's continued existence as an independent monastery. In 1192 Savaric Fitzgeldwin, a career churchman with royal connections, was consecrated Bishop of Bath, the diocese in which Glastonbury was located. Savaric, it seems, had his eye on the abbey from the first; not only did it offer a spiritual eminence in a way that Bath did not, but Glastonbury was arguably the oldest, wealthiest and most prestigious religious house in the kingdom. Through various unsavoury means Savaric obtained the abbacy for himself in 1195, united the monastery to his see and with the approval of Pope Celestine III, Savaric changed his title to Bishop of Bath *and Glastonbury*. Although the monks fought valiantly to retain their monastery's independence, Savaric finally took Glastonbury by force in 1198 when he was enthroned in the abbey church as bishop 'contrary to proper order'.[49] Two years later papal sanction joined the two monasteries in formal union and Glastonbury started a new life as a cathedral-priory, ruled by a bishop.[50]

Notwithstanding continued appeals to Rome over the years that followed all seemed lost for the Glastonbury monks and their supporters. Then, quite unexpectedly, Savaric died in

1205. His successor, Joscelin Troteman a native of Wells, soon decided to abandoned Savaric's struggles with Glastonbury's recalcitrant monks and relinquished his control over the abbey. Joscelin was more interested in claiming the collegiate church at Wells for his diocese, which eventually became the primary seat of the bishopric in 1245 (hence the title Bishop of Bath *and Wells*).[51] But despite abandoning his predecessor's scheme, the final settlement was not formalised until thirteen years into Joscelin's episcopate, when in 1219 Pope Honorius III dissolved the official union of diocese and abbey. Only then did Joscelin drop 'Glastonbury' from his title and after over two decades of struggle, the monks finally regained their independence.

It is difficult to gauge the consequences of Savaric's actions on Glastonbury. For two stormy decades the abbey had housed a bishop's throne and had performed some of the functions of a cathedral church. During this time the abbey's internal affairs were severely disrupted and in regaining its independence, Glastonbury paid dearly, losing both land and privileges. As a result the monks became highly sensitised to both bishop and diocese, and jealous of their rights. Anxious to prove their abbey's spiritual and temporal importance, the community responded with both the acquisition of important new relics and the dissemination of certain documents which left little doubt as to Glastonbury's standing.

During Savaric's rule at Glastonbury, one of the most important events in European history occurred at the other end of the Mediterranean world. In 1204, the Christian city of Constantinople, the capital of the Eastern Roman or Byzantine Empire, fell to the armies of the Fourth Crusade. Originally intended to conquer Muslim-controlled Jerusalem, the crusading armies were diverted by the Venetians to attack the city of Zara in Dalmatia and then Constantinople itself. In the aftermath of the city's fall, Imperial chapels, and Orthodox churches and monasteries were ransacked for loot, but especially religious treasures. The Byzantine emperors had formed great collections of relics gathered from all over the empire and large quantities of sacred objects were now seized and distributed amongst the conquerors, before being shipped west. Some of these relics were given to great churches where they can still be seen today, such as those preserved in the Basilica of San Marco in Venice. Others ended up in far humbler surroundings; one Constantinopolitan relic of the True Cross for example found a new home at the small and impoverished Cluniac Priory of Bromholm on the north Norfolk coast.[52]

In 1212 Eustace Comyn, Glastonbury's sacristan, responsible for the abbey church and its many treasures, approached Peter of Spain, a crusader not long returned from the east. With 'enormous effort and at great expense', Eustace obtained for Glastonbury a spectacular collection of relics which Peter had acquired from a monastery in Constantinople eight years earlier, presumably as plunder. This assemblage consisted of the following astonishing objects:

> Two silver crosses with the wood of the Lord's cross... pieces of the arm of St. Thomas the apostle of India; the jaw and three teeth of St. Philip the apostle and the middle portion of his armbones; a bone of St. Barnabas the apostle and another from the finger of St. John the Baptist; a bone of

St. Luke the evangelist; a bone of St. Mark the evangelist; a thighbone from the leg of St. Stephen the protomartyr; a large bone of St. Lawrence the martyr; a large bone of St. George the martyr; a bone from the head of St. Christopher the martyr; a bone of St. Blaise the martyr; the arm of St. Helen with its flesh and bones, in two pieces; and a bone of St. Scholastica the virgin.[53]

Not only did these relics include the jaw of St Philip, who we may recall was said to have sent the first missionaries to Britain, but also the arm of St Helen or St Helena of Constantinople, the mother of the first Christian emperor, Constantine the Great. Best known for her discovery of the True Cross in Jerusalem in about 327, St Helen was popularly regarded as the daughter of Coel, the mythical founder of Colchester, a British ruler who was later claimed to have been buried in the Old Cemetery at Glastonbury.[54] In 1213, the year after the relics' acquisition, the sanctuary of the great new abbey church of SS Peter and Paul, although far from complete, was formally consecrated. It is not difficult to imagine that these newly acquired relics, which belonged to some of the greatest figures from the early days of Christianity, were prominently displayed or even played a significant role in the proceedings.

Already impressive, Glastonbury's relic collection now easily eclipsed most other churches in South West England. While none of these newly acquired treasures were singled out for particular veneration, such an assemblage, probably still housed in its Byzantine reliquaries will have doubtless helped, bolster perceptions amongst the faithful of Glastonbury's early origins and spiritual importance. Apart from their obvious sanctity as corporeal remains of the blessed, holy relics were also regarded as precious instruments of catechesis – in other words, educational tools for instruction in the faith. Signs of a true event, whose veneration could help the faithful in their prayer and meditation, relics of the holy dead reinforced the salvific value of Christ's ministry and Cross through examples of the saints' lives. Perhaps also regarded as a divine seal of approval for Glastonbury's newly won independence, the very real presence of the apostles and martyrs through their relics must have had a profound impact on all who viewed and venerated them, drawing minds to contemplate the ministry of the apostles and the first days of Christianity.

The second quarter of the thirteenth century also saw the composition of a new document at Glastonbury Abbey, the *carta sancti Patricii episcopi* (Charter of St Patrick the bishop).[55] Supposedly written in the year 430 by St Patrick himself, it was duly copied into new editions of William of Malmesbury's *De Antiquitate*. This gave the charter instant credibility as it could be claimed to have existed before the Great Fire when William had written his history. Although to us an obvious forgery, the *carta sancti Patricii* is significant both for its new claims regarding Glastonbury's foundations and in signalling the newly independent abbey's spiritual aspirations.

The charter opens by stating that after converting the Irish to the faith, Pope Celestine sent Patrick to 'the island of Yniswitrin' where he 'discovered a holy and ancient place chosen by God and consecrated in honour of the undefiled Virgin Mary, the mother of God'. There Patrick 'encountered some brothers, instructed in the rudiments of the catholic faith and pious in their lives, who had succeeded the disciples of the saints Phagan and Deruvian'.[56] Thus from the start it is clear that not only does Glastonbury belong to the Blessed Virgin, but it also supported a monastic community originally established by papal mandate, rather than by a king or bishop and it was the duty of these brothers to serve in St Mary's Church. Having become Glastonbury's first abbot, Patrick was shown 'writings by saints Phagan and Deruvian which asserted that twelve disciples of saints Philip and James had built the old church in honour of our patroness, instructed by the blessed archangel Gabriel; and that moreover the Lord of Heaven had consecrated that church in honour of his mother, while three pagan kings had given twelve portions of land to those twelve for their sustenance.'[57]

Whereas in previous texts, only one apostle, St Philip, had sent missionaries to Glastonbury, he is now joined by St James, a saint whose popularity was growing in the twelfth century through pilgrimage to his shrine at Compostela in Spain. The Virgin's importance is again stressed, as is the royal origin of the first gifts of land to the Old Church. Perhaps most significantly however, Pope Eleutherius' previously unnamed second-century emissaries have now acquired the names 'Phagan and Deruvian', and it is stated that they had rediscovered an ancient church built by the first-century missionaries dispatched to Britain by St Philip. In other words, the two apparently contradictory accounts of Glastonbury's foundation supplied by William of Malmesbury in his *De Antiquitate*, where it was claimed that Glastonbury was both a first- *and* a second-century foundation, have now been brought together in one coherent narrative.

The charter further claims that Patrick took one of the brothers by the name of 'Wellias' with him on an expedition 'through a dense wood to the peak of a hill which rises on that island', in other words, to the top of Glastonbury tor. The name 'Wellias' should be noted here for he is the eponymous founder of the city of Wells. By describing Wellias as a disciple of St Patrick, Glastonbury's first abbot, the charter's author is, of course, characterising the church of Wells, raised again to cathedral status in 1245, as subordinate to Glastonbury. Having reached the tor's summit, Patrick and Wellias discovered a ruined chapel in which was preserved an ancient book. In it had been written the Acts of the Apostles and the deeds of SS Phagan and Deruvian, stating that the papal emissaries had built the oratory 'at the inspiration of our Lord Jesus Christ in honour of St Michael the archangel so that he who would lead men to eternal honour at God's command would there be honoured by men'. Patrick and Wellias remained on the summit praying and fasting during which time they were assailed by 'demons and beasts' before Christ appeared and confirmed that the tor was indeed dedicated to the archangel. This emphasis on God's dedication of the tor to St Michael is particularly noteworthy, for it mirrors the dedication of the Old Church by Christ to His Mother. This suggests that the chapel on the tor was being actively promoted as a pilgrimage site in the early thirteenth century and indulgences, anachronistically incorporated in the charter, would seem to confirm this.

The charter closes by noting that when Patrick finally died, he 'earned burial in the old church to the right of the altar, a place, indicated by an angel, from which a huge flame, visible to all who were present, burst forth'. Although one of the most notorious of Glastonbury forgeries, the *carta sancti Patricii* is an enormously important document in the development of the story of the abbey's origins, for without it, William of Malmesbury's tale of unknown disciples of St Philip coming to Glastonbury might have remained the accepted account of Glastonbury's foundation. Aside from the *carta sancti Patricii*, another supposedly ancient document, the *magnum priviligium regis Inae* (Great Privilege of King Ine), allegedly composed in the year 725, was also altered in the decades following the fire. Possibly a tenth-century forgery or a copy of an earlier legitimate royal text rather than a wholly new creation, the claims it contains are significant. Unlike the *carta sancti Patricii*, which implicitly subjugates the church of Wells to Glastonbury, the reviser of the *priviligium regis Inae* showed no such scruples; here Glastonbury's spiritual authority is writ large.

Ine firstly confirms Glastonbury's ancient possessions, before stating that he keeps watch:

> against the snares of malevolent men and barking dogs, in order that that the church of our Lord Jesus Christ and the ever-virgin Mary, just as it holds first place in the kingdom of Britain and is the fount and origin of all religion, so also may retain the outstanding liberty of its privilege, and in order that she who rules over the angelic choirs in heaven may perform no subservient office for any human being.[58]

Having thus established St Mary's spiritual hegemony at Glastonbury, the privilege goes on to state that the abbey must remain 'untouched by the promulgations and interference of all archbishops and bishops'. Invoking the witness of God, the

Virgin and all the saints, Ine forbids 'the bishop's presumption to establish his Episcopal throne in Glastonbury or the churches subject to it', clearly a sideswipe at the pretentions of Savaric and Joscelin. The king further commands that the bishop and his clerks at Wells shall every year 'acknowledge his mother, the church of Glastonbury' and that the abbot and monks of Glastonbury 'shall receive the sacraments of the Church from any bishop they desire'. In closing, Ine warns the reader that: 'If anyone attempts, furthermore, to pervert or nullify the testament of my generosity and liberty at any future time, upon any occasion, whatever his dignity, profession, or rank, let him know that he will perish with the traitor Judas amidst eternal confusion in the devouring flames of unspeakable torments'.[59] In case the reader retains any doubts regarding the privilege's authority, it is finally noted that in the same year the king granted his charter to the abbey, Ine 'went in person to Rome and brought back the privilege, corroborated by the apostolic seal'.

Although this charter clearly exaggerates Ine's gifts to Glastonbury, it was not written deliberately to deceive its audience. Rather, it documented an already accepted state of affairs and expressed it as an officially written record, albeit retrospectively. Thus, with Patrick's charter and Ine's privilege Glastonbury drew a line in the sand: they 'proved' that the abbey had been anciently gifted its freedom by the highest of spiritual and temporal authorities, and that it should remain free from any control or influence the bishop might bring to bear. Having acquired major relics of the apostles and early martyrs, and disseminated these newly written 'ancient' texts, Glastonbury officially broadcast and reinforced its right to independence to any who might listen. And central to this 'marshalling of antiquity' was by far the most significant addition to the abbey's literary corpus, a text composed in the second quarter of the thirteenth century.

Around the year 1247, for reasons that remain obscure, a new copy of William of Malmesbury's *De Antiquitate* was produced in the abbey scriptorium. To this manuscript an anonymous monkish scribe made a highly significant addition in the form of a wholly new first chapter of his own composition and a rewrite of the second. In this first chapter we are informed that having preached and converted many people in 'the land of the Franks', St Philip made a decision:

> Desiring to spread the word of Christ further he sent twelve of his disciples into Britain to teach the word of life. It is said that he appointed as their leader his very dear friend, Joseph of Arimathea, who had buried the Lord. They came to Britain in 63 AD, the fifteenth year after the assumption of the blessed Mary, and confidently began to preach the faith of Christ.[60]

Here for the first time we learn that the missionaries sent by St Philip were twelve in number and that their leader, 'it is said' (*ut ferant*) was St Joseph of Arimathea. This is the first direct reference which connects Joseph to Glastonbury and so it is in this surprisingly non-committal manner that the saint's name enters the abbey's already well-established body of tradition. [61] The text continues:

After living in that wilderness for a short time the saints were incited by a vision of the archangel Gabriel to build a church in honour of the Virgin Mary, the holy mother of God, in a place that was pointed out to them from heaven. They were not slow to obey this divine command and in the thirty-first year after the passion of the Lord, the fifteenth after the assumption of the glorious Virgin, they completed a chapel as they had been instructed, making the lower part of all its walls of twisted wattle, an unsightly construction no doubt but one adorned by God with many miracles. Since it was the first one in that territory the son of God dignified it with a greater honour by dedicating it in honour of his mother. The twelve saints of whom we have been speaking offered faithful obedience to God and the blessed Virgin in that place, devoting themselves to vigils, fasting and prayers, and were supplied with all necessities by the Virgin's aid and, as the pious believe, by a vision of her.[62]

Throughout this passage St Mary's importance to Glastonbury is made abundantly clear to the reader. Ordained by God through a vision of the archangel Gabriel, the twelve saints (mirroring the twelve apostles of Christ) establish the first church at Glastonbury and are assisted in their endeavours by the Virgin. We should also note the last sentence which states that the pious believed that St Mary had appeared at Glastonbury in a vision. This is the only mention of such an occurrence in the abbey's history and it is useful as it helps us understand the nature of Christ's dedication of the church to

His Mother. If the dedication is not meant to be understood as a literal or visionary happening, then presumably the author must have intended a spiritual understanding on the reader's part. More than the presence of Christ in the sacrament of the Mass or the Holy Spirit amongst the faithful, Christ's dedication of Glastonbury's first church was a mystical act, in much the same way as Westminster Abbey claimed to have been miraculously consecrated by St Peter in the seventh century.[63] This interpretation is seemingly supported in the rewritten second chapter in which it is stated that when SS Phagan and Deruvian found the Old Church, 'the Architect of Heaven showed by many miracles and sacred mysteries that He had consecrated it to Himself and Mary, the holy mother of God' and that the two saints, 'inferred from a heavenly oracle that the Lord had especially chosen that place before all others in Britain to invoke the name of his glorious mother'.[64] Thus, having established beyond doubt both Christ's and the Virgin's intimate association with Glastonbury, and having finally identified an appropriate original founder in the person of the undeniably biblical Joseph of Arimathea, the abbey's future was assured.

Chapter 5: The House of the Virgin

In the century which followed Glastonbury's recovery of independence from the bishopric, the abbey grew and prospered, helped by a succession of able and prudent abbots. One of the most powerful monastic foundations in England, it consolidated its huge estates, enjoyed immense wealth, received numerous privileges, was associated with many prominent saints and claimed to be the most ancient Christian foundation in the realm. Then, quite unexpectedly, during the abbacy of Adam of Sodbury (1323-1334) a miraculous event occurred in the Lady Chapel:

> Once, while the convent of Glastonbury was chanting the antiphon *Salve regina* in devotion to God and blessed Mary, the glorious Virgin's image which stood at the altar moved like a living lady. While a whole crowd of secular people looked on, and while the monks watched as well, she clapped for the child she held on her lap, now putting her hand to his face, now drawing it back in reverence; nor did she cease these movements until the choir had haltingly sung through the whole antiphon.[65]

This miracle was first recorded by the Glastonbury monk Edmund Stourton, in his lost book *De nominibus Ihesu et Marie* (The Name of Jesus and Mary), which he addressed to Pope John XXII (1316-1334).[66] Although we only know of Stourton's

Fig. 7. A small statue of St Mary found in the
abbey ruins (after Warner 1826).

book and the account of the miracle it contained from a later reference, works such as his indicate that Glastonbury's monks had a lively enthusiasm for the Virgin's cult and that they zealously promulgated it at the very highest levels beyond the confines of their monastery. It seems that this miracle deeply affected Abbot Sodbury, for it was later recorded that he not only 'adorned the high altar [of the abbey church] with a large statue of the Mother of God and a magnificent tabernacle', but in February 1333 he also instituted a body of eight secular priests whose primary purpose was to 'minister daily in the Lady Chapel' and serve in the charnel Chapel of St Michael which stood on the south side of the Old Cemetery.[67] The most important development in the devotional life of the abbey since the reordering after the Great Fire of 1184, Abbot Sodbury's initiative seems likely to have been a direct result of increased pilgrim traffic to the Lady Chapel in the wake of the miracle of the moving statue.

Later collectively known as the 'Clerks of Our Lady',[68] these priests' daily routine mirrored the Canonical Hours of the monks' Divine Office – Nocturns, Matins, Lauds, Prime, Terce, Sext, Nones, Vespers and Compline. In addition to observing this formal timetable of prayer, the clerks were also expected to celebrate their own masses, the Office for the Dead and join the monastic community in worship on certain festivals. Provided with a house and garden close to the Lady Chapel, by the Dissolution in 1539 there were seemingly twelve clerks[69] – doubtless intentionally mirroring St Joseph's twelve original companions. Acting almost like a monastery within a monastery, these priests served in a church in which it was believed that the

Virgin, in a very tangible way, had made evident her continued support for Glastonbury.

Only a decade or so after the miracle in the Lady Chapel, the increasingly elaborate story of the abbey's sacred origins was recorded by a Glastonbury monk commonly known as 'John of Glastonbury', although his name was probably John Seen.[70] A well-known historian, John had spent time at Oxford where he had received the degree of Doctor of Theology by 1360. Completing his history of Glastonbury Abbey by *circa* 1342, the *Cronica sive Antiquitates Glastoniensis Ecclesie* (The Chronicle of Ancient Church of Glastonbury) sets out to be a comprehensive history of the monastery from the earliest times to the author's own day and was written to update William of Malmesbury's *De Antiquitate*. Although his chronicle is highly derivative, John appears to have read widely and conducted detailed research, as his work has been described as 'a masterpiece of neatly interconnecting links'.[71] Much like Malmesbury's *De Antiquitate*, the earliest surviving copy of John's chronicle was written some time after the original volume's completion and the initial portion of the work which contains most of the references to Glastonbury's origins is absent. Later copies of the manuscript which include this missing section also incorporate a number of additions which are difficult to date. In consequence we are not wholly sure what John himself wrote, but we can be certain that the new material the *Cronica* contains dates from no earlier than the second quarter of the fourteenth century.

The introduction – possibly written by someone other than John – has a lengthy, but revealing title: 'On the antiquity of the ancient church of St Mary at Glastonbury; and on the addition which St David made to it, at the insistence of divine revelation, and which he dedicated to the honour of blessed Mary.' From the outset it is thus clearly signalled that Glastonbury is a place of special importance to the Virgin and, as the book proceeds, it rapidly becomes clear that the ethos of John's work is essentially Marian. As James Carley has observed, John's account of fourteenth-century developments at Glastonbury is particularly valuable as it is not retrospective, but rather 'it represents his immediate response to personally witnessed events',[72] It is quite possible that John had been present during the miraculous occurrence in the Lady Chapel or at the very least knew people who were. The Marian tone of John's chronicle is thus both explicable and understandable. Indeed, it would be surprising if the Virgin's presence was not felt throughout the work.

In the prologue which follows the introduction, John dedicates the *Cronica* to his fellow monks who live 'under the quiet protection and direction of our advocate Mary the blessed and ever-virgin Mother of God'[73] and he later comments that Glastonbury is rightly called the 'source and origin' of all religion in England'. Significantly, in John's mind this was not because of any association with St Joseph of Arimathea, but 'because of the Old Church of Glastonbury, which was the first sign of Christianity in this land' and on account of St Dunstan and St Aethelwold 'and the many other saints who sprang from that same church [i.e. Glastonbury] to spread religion throughout the kingdom'.[74] The sanctity of Glastonbury therefore is not restricted to its foundation, although it is important, but in its continuing role as a centre of evangelisation and Christian culture.

Glastonbury: Origins of the Sacred

In his first chapter John clearly, almost triumphantly, proclaims Glastonbury's status:

> No other human hands made the church of Glaston, but Christ's disciples founded and built it by angelic doctrine, an unattractive structure, certainly, but adorned by God with manifold virtue; the High Priest of the Heavens himself, the maker and redeemer of humankind, our Lord Jesus Christ, in his true presence dedicated it to himself and to his most holy mother. On account of its antiquity the English called this church the 'ealdechirche' - that is, 'the Old Church' – and it is quite evident that the men of that region hold no oath more sacred or binding than one on the Old Church – and they shun nothing through fear of punishment for their crime more than perjury. Glastonbury, originally built of wattles, is first and eldest of all churches in England.[75]

John also applies the epithet 'Second Rome' to Glastonbury and qualifies its use, stating: 'Just as the place is founded upon a great and ancient reverence, so it towers mightily in the privilege of its sanctity. Indeed, it is called a second Rome, for just as the city of Rome is distinguished by a multitude of holy martyrs, so also that church [Glastonbury] is held venerable for the multitude of holy confessors who rest there.'[76] Significantly, a near contemporary papal bull dated November 1332 from Pope John XXII to Ralph, Bishop of Bath, records that King Edward III had recently visited Glastonbury 'on account of the multitude of martyrs there buried'.[77] Clearly Glastonbury's reputation was well known.

The House of the Virgin

In the *Cronica*'s fourteenth chapter, John discusses Glastonbury's virtues as a place of burial, echoing William of Malmesbury by claiming that: 'The chief personages of the country would rather await the day of resurrection in the monastery of Glastonbury, in the protection of Mary the ever-virgin Mother of God, than anywhere else – a great indication how venerable the spot is to them.'[78] Later in the same chapter, John provides further reasons why the 'holy earth is so eagerly desired for Christian burial. The first reason is that the Lord dedicated it in his own presence for the burial of his servants. Second, the Lord is thought to concede a great remission of sins to all those who are buried here, or elsewhere with some portion of this holy earth, for the sake of the prayers and merits of the saints who rest there. Third, because masses and other prayers are said daily on their behalf.'[79] Thus, Glastonbury's appeal to the faithful rests not just in its special relationship with the Virgin, but to Christ, His saints and the continual intercession at the abbey which is made by the living on behalf of the dead.

We should also observe that St Joseph of Arimathea as Glastonbury's putative founder not only makes frequent appearances throughout John's chronicle, but that it is the earliest work to set out the abbey's fully formulated Joseph legend. According to the various sources on which John relied, Joseph was 'appointed guardian of the blessed ever-virgin Mary by blessed John the apostle, while John himself laboured at preaching to the Ephesians: Joseph was present at the Assumption of the same glorious Virgin, along with blessed Philip and his other disciples, and he preached incessantly through many lands the things which he had heard and seen of the Lord Jesus Christ and his mother Mary' before being miraculously transported to Britain.[80] Much of what follows John simply lifts from William of Malmesbury's *De Antiquitate*, noting that the Archangel Gabriel appeared and commanded that a church be built in the Virgin's honour, that Joseph and his companions lived pious lives until the last of the company died. After this time: 'the spot which had previously been a dwelling of saints then became a den of wild beasts, until it pleased the blessed Virgin to restore her oratory to the memory of the faithful'.[81]

In both the fourteenth and twenty-first chapter of the *Cronica*, John incorporates the enigmatic 'Prophesy of Melkin', a text whose introduction constitutes a pivotal moment in Glastonbury's literary history. Melkin was supposedly a Welsh bard whose greatness rivalled Merlin's and pre-dated him by a number of years. Melkin's prophesy is the earliest surviving text which claims that St Joseph of Arimathea was actually buried at the abbey. While no modern scholar seriously accepts Melkin's literal existence as an historical figure and the prophesy as it currently stands can have been written no earlier than the mid-thirteenth century, James Carley has argued that it may contain earlier material.[82] Be this as it may, a literal 'Melkin' – Glastonbury's great Arthurian sage – was accepted as an historical figure throughout the Middle Ages and his prophesy was treated seriously. David Townsend's translation runs as follows:

> The Isle of Avalon, greedy in the burial of pagans,
> above others in the world, decorated at the burial
> place of all of them with vaticinatory little spheres

of prophesy, and in future it will be adorned with those who praise the Most High. Abbadare, powerful in Saphat, most noble of pagans, took his sleep there with 104,000. Amongst them Joseph de Marmore, named 'of Arimathea', took everlasting sleep. And he lies on a forked line close to the southern corner of the chapel with prepared wattle above the powerful and venerable Maiden, the thirteen aforesaid sphered things occupying the place. For Joseph has with him in the tomb two white and silver vessels filled with the blood and sweat of the prophet Jesus. When his tomb is found, it will be seen whole and undefiled in the future, and will be open to all the earth. From then on, neither water nor heavenly dew will be able to be lacking for those who inhabit the most noble island. For a long time before the Day of Judgement in Josephat will these things be open and declared to the living.[83]

The meaning of this curious passage has been much debated, in particular the 'spheres of prophesy' which may or may not relate to the Old Church's enigmatic pavement mentioned by William of Malmesbury. More important for us, however, are the relics Joseph carries with him and what their deposition in Britain implies. As Carley has observed: 'In this cryptic text the mysterious Holy Grail of Arthurian romance tradition has been transformed into a wholly respectable Holy Blood relic, historically unimpeachable, brought to England by Joseph of Arimathea.'[84] St Joseph now arrives in Glastonbury with Christ's 'blood and sweat' which, of course, mirrors the wine and water mixed and consecrated at Mass. Joseph and the relics he bears can thus be read as the coming of Catholic orthodoxy to British shores. Indeed, throughout the *Cronica*, Joseph's intimate association with Christ, the Virgin and the apostles is stressed, while his traditional biblical role in the crucifixion drama undoubtedly helped foster the growing devotion to Christ's Passion which characterised the later Middle Ages. While the tone of Melkin's prophesy is undeniably mysterious, it none the less sits within the Catholic mainstream.

Finally, we should also note that John honours Glastonbury with a new title in the second chapter of his *Cronica*. Firstly he quotes from Geoffrey of Monmouth's *Vita Merlini* (Life of Merlin) written *circa* 1150, which links the otherworldly 'Island of Apples' with Glastonbury:

> The island of apples, which is called fortunate, is truly named, for it brings forth all things of its own accord. It needs no farmers to till the fields, and there is no cultivation save that which nature provides. It freely brings forth fertile stalks and grapes, and apples born of precious seed in its forests. The earth nourishes all things, as bounteous as tended land; one lives there a hundred years or more.

Having established this correspondence, John adds the following lines:

> This was the new Jerusalem, the faith's refinement, a holy hill, celebrated as the ladder of heaven. He scarcely pays the penalties of hell who lies buried here.[85]

The House of the Virgin

In this way John again highlights the salvific properties of burial in Glastonbury's sacred soil and with such emotive and multi-layered language as this employed throughout the *Cronica*, the reader is left in little doubt as to Glastonbury's unique spiritual status in England. While Canterbury boasted a metropolitan archbishop, Westminster was the royal coronation and burial church and St Alban's abbey possessed the body of the British proto-martyr, it was Glastonbury and Glastonbury alone which had been chosen by God, dedicated to His Mother and established by a man popularly believed throughout the Middle Ages to have been Christ's step-uncle. Inevitably, such an extraordinary claim was to have extraordinary repercussions.

Chapter 6: St Joseph of Glastonbury

The middle years of the fourteenth century saw awareness of St Joseph of Arimathea as Glastonbury's founder begin to manifest outside the confines of the abbey. Probably as the result of the dissemination of John's *Cronica*, in 1345 one John Blome of London was empowered by King Edward III or his chancellor to search for St Joseph's grave at Glastonbury. Blome had seemingly received some sort of spiritual revelation as the royal writ states that 'a divine injunction has been laid on him as concerning the venerable body of the noble Decurion Joseph of Arimathea, which rests in Christ buried within the bounds of the monastery of Glastonbury and is to be revealed in these days to the honour [of God?] and the edification of many'.[86] Although in 1367, some twenty two-years after the event, an anonymous East Anglian chronicler reported that: 'The bodies of Joseph of Arimathea and his companions were found at Glastonbury', there is no contemporary evidence that confirms that Blome actually conducted his search and the complete silence from the abbey would seem to confirm that he had not.

But despite the diffusion of John's *Cronica* and its claims regarding Joseph's burial at Glastonbury, the abbey by no means exercised a monopoly over the saint or his earthly remains. By the fourteenth century the cathedrals of Canterbury and Durham, and the priories of Tynemouth and Christchurch all possessed Arimathean relics in their collections, but none of these

Fig. 8. The arms of St Joseph of Arimathea. Carved on an early sixteenth-century bench end in St Michael's Parish Church, North Cadbury, Somerset.

monasteries had direct links to Glastonbury or its traditions. Nor did they attempt to foster particular devotion to St Joseph within their walls. It seems likely that these relics reached England directly from the Holy Land, Rome or Constantinople and, as with so many other obscure Biblical relics scattered throughout Christendom, they simply added to the sanctity of the churches in which they were preserved. The fact that they were not linked to Glastonbury or its traditions is telling; presumably Joseph's English connections were either unknown or considered too unimportant to be worth highlighting.[87]

It was not until the beginning of the fifteenth century that Glastonbury would recognise the unrealised potential of its sub-apostolic founder. Around the year 1400, the *Magna Tabula* (Great Tablet) was erected in the abbey church at Glastonbury. Consisting of six vellum sheets mounted on four large wooden leaves hinged like a book, this remarkable object measuring approximately three feet by one and a half feet survived the dissolution of the abbey in 1539 and is preserved today in the Bodleian Library in Oxford. Probably commissioned by Abbot John Chinnock (1375-1420), the *Tabula*'s nearly 600 lines of text are divided into numerous short 'chapters'. Mostly taken from the abbey's earlier chronicles, the text is almost exclusively devoted to Glastonbury's origins and early history, and its format and contents suggest a deliberate attempt to promote and publicise Joseph of Arimathea's role in the abbey's story. There are, however, two small but significant additions to this old material. Firstly, a list of indulgences, totalling sixty-four years and one hundred and ninety-seven days, which pilgrims could gain from visiting the abbey and secondly, a short 'chapter' concerning the charnel Chapel of St Michael in the Old Cemetery, which stood to the south of the Lady Chapel.

According to the *Tabula* many relics had been stored under the altar of the charnel chapel, despite it being an ancient and dilapidated structure. Then in 1382 Abbot Chinnock restored the chapel and added to its dedication; it was no longer simply the Chapel of St Michael, but the Chapel of St Michael 'and St Joseph and all the saints resting in the cemetery' (*et Ioseph et sanctorum in cimiterio requiescentium*).[88] The chapel's restoration and rededication included the erection of a life-size Deposition group in its interior which probably stood behind the altar and acted as a reredos. Depicting Christ's descent from the cross in which Joseph traditionally played a key role, we can be reasonably certain that the saint's figure would have been given particular prominence. We should also note that the abbot's choice of the charnel chapel for dedication to Joseph was a peculiarly appropriate one; not only had Joseph given up his tomb for Christ and lay buried somewhere in the cemetery, but St Michael, often chosen as patron of cemeteries, was believed to bring men's souls to judgement and protect the faithful from the enemy. The 'noble Decurion' and the archangel were an ideal coupling. As this chapel's restoration and improvement project demonstrates, Abbot Chinnock actively promoted St Joseph's cult at Glastonbury. No longer just a name, confined to an obscure historical text like the papal missionaries St Phagan or St Deruvian, Joseph now stepped off the page and became a living presence in the monastery's devotional life; monks and pilgrims alike could now seek his intercession by praying in the newly refurbished cemetery chapel named in his honour.

Just as important as the charnel chapel's restoration, the *Tabula* also tells us that Abbot Chinnock worked on the Lady Chapel, where he 'eventually clothed this image [the ancient 'miraculous' statue of St Mary] as befitted it, adorning it with gold and precious stones and enclosing many relics within it'. The image's new appearance, clad with precious materials, would clearly heighten its profile in the Lady Chapel, stressing its status as the building's principal devotional aid and visual focus. To the medieval mind, the gold and gems used to adorn the image served as material analogues of the Virgin's spiritual glorification. Abbot Chinnock's enclosure of holy relics within the image is also noteworthy. A not uncommon practice throughout the Middle Ages, the relics, unseen by human eyes, further guaranteed the holiness and authenticity of the statue, and the altar which it adorned. More than this, like the Lady Chapel it inhabited, the image of the Virgin became simultaneously relic and reliquary, the vessel of salvation. As God Himself had been enclosed in the Virgin's womb, so the relics of the saints were enclosed in an image of St Mary the Virgin, symbolic of the Church enclosing and sheltering the saints, just as the Lady Chapel enclosed and sheltered the faithful – a complex multi-layered symbolism which would not have been lost on her monastic audience, even if not fully appreciated by the average pilgrim.

At roughly the same time as these restorations were going on and the *Magna Tabula* was erected inside the abbey church, a free-standing stone pillar, known as the Pillar of St David, was built to the north of the Lady Chapel upon which was affixed a brass plate.[89] This pillar's function was to act as a permanent

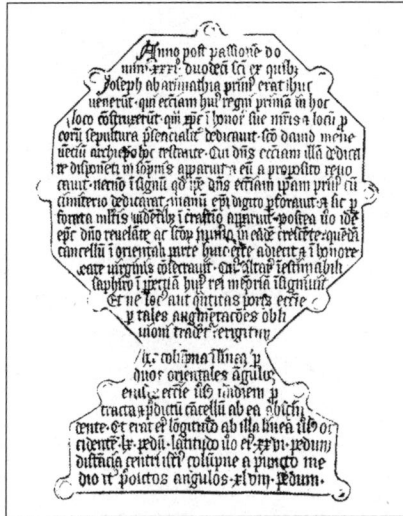

Fig. 9. The brass plate from the Pillar of
St David, which stood to the north
of the Lady Chapel.

memorial, marking the original eastern extent of the ancient wooden church which Joseph had built and the text inscribed on the brass plate made this clear. The Latin inscription started with the following lines: 'The 31st year after the Passion of the Lord twelve saints, among whom Joseph of Arimathea was the first, came here. They built in this place that church, the first in this realm, which Christ in honour of his Mother, and the place for their burial, presently dedicated.'[90] It is therefore clear that by the beginning of the fifteenth century Christ's consecration of the Old Church and St Joseph's role as Glastonbury's founder were clearly and unambiguously signalled – quite literally – on the ground.

Glastonbury: Origins of the Sacred

On the wider European stage, Glastonbury and Joseph also appeared in the spotlight. This was due to English involvement in a pan-European attempt to reform and strengthen the Catholic Church in the first thirty years of the fifteenth century. Asserting that ultimate authority in spiritual matters resided not in the single person of the pope, but with the Universal Church as a corporation of Christians, embodied by a general church council, the Conciliar movement was a response to the papal captivity at Avignon. This was the period (1309-1376) when the popes were removed from Rome and subjected to political pressure from the kings of France.

The schism which ensued (between 1378 and 1417 there were two, then three rival popes) was one of the primary causes of the summoning of Councils at Pisa (1409), Constance (1417), Pavia-Siena (1424) and Basel (1434). One of the major issues at these councils was the notion of nationhood – that the rule of Christian nations should take precedence over law issued from the papal curia in Rome. This of course meant that not only did kingdoms have to demonstrate that they constituted *natios*, but also that the dates of foundation of various national churches had to be established to determine their precedence in councils. At the Council of Pisa, Bishop Hallum of Salisbury claimed that England deserved parity with the other *natios* of the Catholic Church due to its apostolic conversion by St Joseph of Arimathea, the founder of Glastonbury. But it was at the Council of Constance in 1417, at which the schism was finally resolved, that Glastonbury made its most significant appearance. The French delegates at the council claimed that the English church was small, riven with heresy and had received the faith later than the kingdom of France and was thus not worthy of nationhood.

The English delegation's riposte was delivered by Thomas Polton, later appointed Bishop of Worcester.[91] Polton claimed that, when compared with France, the English nation 'also known as the British nation' was 'superior in the antiquity of its faith, dignity and honour and at least equal in all the divine gifts of regal power and numbers and wealth of clergy and people'. Many saints had been born in England, most notably St Helena and her son, the emperor Constantine the Great, 'born in the royal city of York'. Thus power, influence and riches of the Roman Church and the enlightenment it had brought to the world might be attributed directly to the blessed realm of the English. The conversion of the Roman Empire, the endowment of the church, the building of St Peter's Basilica in Rome and the finding of the True Cross were thus all attributed to the acts of an 'English' man and woman.

Regarding the arrival of the faith in England, Polton stated:

> For immediately after Christ's passion Joseph of Arimathea, a noble Decurion, who took Christ down from the cross, came to England with twelve companions as to a vineyard to be cultivated early for the Lord, and converted the people to the faith. The king gave them twelve hides of land, and assigned the diocese of Bath as their livelihood. They are buried in the abbey of Glastonbury, in the diocese of Bath, according to written testimony, and that abbey is known to have been endowed from early times with those twelve hides.[92]

Glastonbury: Origins of the Sacred

As Joseph and his companions are claimed to have arrived in England 'immediately after Christ's passion', this of course meant that England was a Christian nation long before France. Moreover, 'that puissant English royal house never strayed from the obedience of the church of Rome, but until this day has always fought for it in exemplary Christian fashion'. Thus Glastonbury was internationally recognised as the place where Christianity first took root in England. Although Westminster Abbey was the English royal coronation and burial church, the English monarchy's intimate link with Glastonbury, having given the land for the establishment of the Catholic faith, was thus clearly signalled. Moreover, as Valerie Lagorio has observed, in consequence of English involvement in the Conciliar movement, 'St Joseph of Arimathea and Glastonbury received international recognition, which fully transformed him from a local monastic legend into an English national saint.'[93]

In the light of the presence of both the Bishop of Bath and Wells, and two consecutive abbots of Glastonbury at all four church councils, it is hardly surprising that St Joseph's newly won fame and importance had a further impact on the ground at Glastonbury.[94] We know this was the case from the single surviving copy of a letter written by Abbot Nicholas Frome (1420-1456) to King Henry V (reigned 1413-1422) contained in a manuscript preserved in the Apostolic Library in Vatican City. Seemingly, this letter was written by the abbot in response to what must have been a forceful request from the king that St Joseph's burial place at Glastonbury should now be found. As a result of the king's request, some sort of excavation did occur at Glastonbury in 1419 when it was claimed that remarkable discoveries had been made. Significantly, the abbot's letter to the king does not actually state that the bodies of St Joseph and his companions had been discovered; rather, Abbot Frome tells the story of his abbey's origins before recounting the discoveries made during the excavations, leaving the reader to make a direct association between the two.

According to Abbot Frome's letter, investigation in the southern part of the Old Cemetery (in other words, the area in which SS Michael and Joseph's charnel chapel stood), revealed three coffins buried at a depth of fourteen feet. In two of the coffins were found the bones of single individuals (presumably meant to be taken as SS Phagan and Deruvian) and in the third

Fig. 10. St Joseph of Arimathea as represented on fifteenth-century glass in the east window of All Saints' Parish Church, Langport, Somerset.

the complete relics of a further twelve individuals (presumably the twelve original missionaries who accompanied St Joseph). Within St Michael's Chapel itself, under the southern corner of the altar a final coffin was discovered, 'with the bones of a decayed man. This coffin was adorned most excellently beyond the others, with linen cloth inside all over. And because it excelled all the others in delicacy of scent and eminence of place it was enclosed in another large coffin until clearer notice of it will be able to be had in the future.'[95] (The contents of this final coffin were presumably meant to be understood as the remains of St Joseph himself.) Thus it seems that the stage was set for a royal visitation of the abbey by Henry V - presumably at which the relics would have been publically unveiled and translated to the abbey church amidst great pomp - but the king died before any such plan could come to fruition and the moment was lost.

Chapter 7: The Final Flowering

Sadly, it is impossible to say what effect all this activity and interest in the abbey's origins had on the complex of monastic buildings at Glastonbury. Barring the chance survival of a couple of late medieval depictions of St Joseph in parish churches, we know nothing of how Glastonbury's origins were depicted visually at the monastery as the interior decoration of the great church is a total loss.[96] Medieval Catholicism was an intensely visual culture and this is all too easily forgotten today. Wall paintings, stained glass, liturgical furnishings and vestments were all destroyed in the decades after the Dissolution. Although we can reasonably assume that the story of Glastonbury's origins was visually displayed alongside dedicatory, explanatory and devotional texts, they are impossible to reconstruct and we have no way of gauging their impact or influence on those who saw them. We are on slightly safer ground, however, if we turn to surviving literary sources which address Glastonbury's putative foundation.

During the century before the Dissolution, literary interest in St Joseph grew slowly. Prior to this time, the saint was conspicuous by his absence in both English and European literature; Matthew Paris, for example, did not mention St Joseph in his *Chronica Majora* (Great Chronicle) and the saint is equally absent from Jacob of Voragine's *Legenda Aurea*

(Golden Legend), the most influential collection of saints' lives produced in the Middle Ages. While Joseph did feature in English biblical narratives and images of the crucifixion, such as that which appears in the 'Holkham Bible', he was not given particular prominence or linked with Glastonbury.[97] At the abbey itself, the situation is difficult to assess as so little written evidence weathered the Dissolution. However, one chance survival, a mid-fifteenth century miscellany preserved at Trinity College, Cambridge, contains nearly ninety Latin and English texts collected by a Glastonbury monk, including a hymn and collect to the two St Josephs (of Nazareth and Arimathea).[98] Probably written at the abbey *circa* 1450, the two Josephs, referred to as 'senior' and 'junior', are praised, the latter for bearing the corpse of Christ to the holy sepulchre with the aid of the St Mary whom he 'served and loved', and as the founder of the first church at Glastonbury where he 'preached the joy of both' Son and Mother – Christ and the Virgin. This hymn's chance survival demonstrates that at least one member of the Glastonbury community had an active devotion to his founder, having written the hymn, while another thought it worth copying. It seems highly likely therefore that similar material was produced and that it has been lost to us.

Be this as it may, outside the abbey Joseph mostly appeared in secular fiction rather than devotional writing and even then infrequently. John Hardyng's *Chronicle* for example, completed in 1465, offered a fantastical amalgam of Glastonbury traditions and the Galahad grail quest in which Joseph featured while, in 1485, Caxton published Thomas Malory's works under the title *Le Morte d'Arthur* and although neither Joseph nor Glastonbury feature in the main text, the connection between Arthur and Glastonbury was pointed out by Caxton in his preface. It had to wait until the third and final edition of the *Nova Legenda Angliae* (New English Legendary) printed in 1516 that a 'life' of Joseph appeared in devotional literature. The *De Sancto Joseph ab Armathia* (The Saint Joseph of Arimathea), extracted entirely from John of Glastonbury's *Cronica*, included no new details concerning Glastonbury's sacred origins, but it gained Joseph and Glastonbury national recognition at a popular level.

It may well have been this growing literary awareness of St Joseph which encouraged the expansion of the saint's cult at Glastonbury towards the end of the fifteenth century. At this time an enormously complicated and disruptive building scheme was undertaken at the west end of the abbey church. The vaulting of the Lady Chapel was taken down, an enormous hole was then dug beneath the chapel in which a new crypt in an old-fashioned architectural style was constructed, before the Lady Chapel was re-roofed and put back into service. This new crypt was used as a chapel dedicated solely to St Joseph of Arimathea; presumably the Chapel of SS Michael and Joseph in the Old Cemetery was becoming too cramped. Now pilgrims to Glastonbury could not only enter the Lady Chapel and venerate the 'miraculous' image of the Virgin, but they could descend to the crypt and, in a pseudo-ancient environment, venerate a statue of Glastonbury's sub-apostolic founder. Conceivably those who did so imagined themselves close to the spot where the saint and his companions worshipped when they arrived in the first century.

Glastonbury: Origins of the Sacred

This substantial new crypt chapel has traditionally been attributed to Glastonbury's penultimate abbot, Richard Beere (1493-1524). An energetic Renaissance man, Abbot Beere built extensively at Glastonbury, liberally embellishing both church and cloistral complex. His building works, listed by John Leland shortly before the Dissolution, included new lodgings for the Clerks of Our Lady and a chapel dedicated to the Holy Sepulchre of Christ which served as the abbot's chantry after his death. A chapel dedicated to Our Lady of Loreto was also constructed. This was the focus of a fashionable Italian devotion which centred on the holy house of Nazareth (the childhood home of Christ) which the abbot had encountered while travelling in Italy on royal business. Commissioning three copies of John of Glastonbury's *Cronica*, which he had brought up to date with a continuation to his own day, Abbot Beere introduced lectures on classical authors (*Lectura antique operis*[99]) for the monastic community, corresponded with the humanist scholar Erasmus and even used a classical intaglio in his personal seal ring.[100]

Abbot Beere also had a shield of arms created for Joseph using the saint's emblems - a white ground with drops of blood scattered on it, divided by a green knotted cross, flanked by golden ampoules on either side. Clearly interested in the visual idioms of humanism, other Glastonbury shields of arms were seemingly designed at the same time. A number of these devices were used on corbels in St Benignus' (now St Benedict's) Church in Glastonbury which Abbot Beere rebuilt. One of these corbels bears a caduceus, the emblem of the Roman deity Mercury, the messenger of the gods. But in this case the central wand around which two snakes were traditionally entwined has been replaced

The Final Flowering

by a bishop's or mitred abbot's crosier, thus creating a suitable symbol for Joseph as messenger of god, the Christian Mercury, who brought the good news of the Christian faith to the shores of Britain in the first century.

It was in this context of dynamism and creativity at the abbey that the last medieval source addressing Glastonbury's sacred origins, the verse, *Lyfe of Joseph of Armathia,*[sic]was written at the beginning of the sixteenth century. [101] Perhaps commissioned by Abbot Beere, it was printed in London by Richard Pynson in 1520. Although the *Lyfe*'s author remains anonymous, he is thought to have been a Glastonbury monk. A simple pamphlet meant for easy sale and distribution, its production clearly illustrates Glastonbury's self-promotion as both as the birth-place of English Christianity and as an important pilgrimage centre.

The early part of the poem is based on the familiar version of St Joseph's life taken from the narrative in John of Glastonbury's *Cronica* although there are a few significant additions. Most importantly in this respect is the blood of Christ which 'in two curettes Ioseph did take' at the crucifixion and which then accompanied him on his wanderings. Having travelled from the Holy Land to Britain, Joseph and his companions eventually settle in 'au[i]longe' (Avalon), 'Nowe called Glastonbury' which was given to them by the local pagan ruler, Arviragus. What they then did is summarised by two verses of enormous importance to both the development of the abbey's foundation legend and to perceptions of Glastonbury as England's premier holy site. Although the *Lyfe* was written to emphasise Joseph's role as the monastery's founder and extol his intercessory potency at the abbey, these two verses clearly signal not only the close

71

connection between Joseph of Arimathea and the Virgin but, more importantly, a shift in emphasis in the presentation of St Mary's cult at Glastonbury. Although difficult to decipher, they repay close examination.

> There Ioseph lyued with other hermyttes twelfe,
> That were the chyfe of all the company,
> But Ioseph was the chefe hym-selfe;
> There led they an holy lyfe and gostely.
> Tyll, at the last, Ihesu the mighty,
> He sent to Ioseph thaungell gabryell,
> Which bad hym, as the writing doth specify,
> Of our ladyes assumpeyon to bylde a chapel.
>
> So Ioseph dyd as the aungell hym bad,
> And Wrought there an ymage of our lady;
> For to serue hyr great deuocion he had,
> And that same ymage is yet at Glastenbury,
> In the same churche; there ye may it se.
> For it was the first, as I vnderstande,
> That euer was sene in this countre;
> For Ioseph it made with his owne hande.[102]

Not only is the *Lyfe*'s author clearly reasserting Glastonbury's pre-eminence as the earliest and most important shrine of the Virgin in the British Isles but just as significantly, the statue of St Mary is now presented as a type of image known in Greek as an *acheiropoietos*, i.e. 'not made by ordinary human hands'.[103] Such images were extremely uncommon in the medieval world and were held in high esteem.[104] Believed to have been created miraculously or to have been painted or carved from life, often by St Luke the Evangelist, they were regarded as sacred from their very creation; they became relics in their own right, quite aside from any later miraculous occurrences associated with them.

The Final Flowering

In this respect, Glastonbury's ancient statue of St Mary took on a whole new dimension. Claimed to have been carved at angelic prompting by St Joseph himself, who not only knew the Virgin in life but was also considered Christ's step-uncle, at a stroke, Glastonbury's statue was seen to transcend all other images of St Mary in England. It thus became a unique object of pilgrimage which underlined the abbey's sanctity.[105] The *Lyfe*'s author links the existing Lady Chapel with Joseph's first church by stating that they were 'the same churche'.[106] He also notes that the Lady Chapel was dedicated to the Assumption of Our Lady, thereby associating both the chapel and the image with what had become the most important Marian feast of the Middle Ages. At a stroke this promoted Glastonbury's Lady Chapel into the feast's primary devotional *locus* in England – effectively implying that if you wished to celebrate Our Lady's Assumption, then you should do so at Glastonbury.[107]

The *Lyfe* then recounts Joseph's death and burial at Glastonbury, before listing the miracles wrought through his intervention in 1503. This section ends by stating that learned men may consult the books of Glastonbury, such as St David's *Life*, which prove that Glastonbury is the 'holyest erth of england' as 'our lorde it hallowed with his owne hande'.[108] The final three verses list two 'meruaylles' (marvels) which could be seen as evidence of God's grace in Glastonbury. Firstly, a walnut tree which did not come into leaf until St Barnabas' Day (11 June), which stood in the Old Cemetery close to the Lady Chapel, and secondly, three hawthorn trees which stood on 'Werall' (Weary-all Hill) and which 'burge and bere grene leaues' at Christmastide. It is important here to notice that although this is the earliest literary reference to the famous Glastonbury or Holy Thorn, there is no direct link made between the hawthorn and Joseph, or the saint's arrival in Glastonbury – that would have to wait until *after* the Dissolution. The *Lyfe* concludes with 'A Praysyng to Joseph', seven verses extolling the 'tresour of Glastenbury moost imperyall' and his virtues as a healer of the sick and as intercessor at the heavenly throne.[109] This *Lyfe* of St Joseph represents the final flowering of the Catholic foundation legend before the Dissolution overtook the abbey.

On 14th November 1539, Richard Whiting, the last Abbot of Glastonbury was subjected to a show trial at the Bishop's Palace in Wells. Found guilty of treason, the following day the abbot was taken to Glastonbury where he and two of his monks were hung, drawn and quartered on the summit of the Tor. Although 15th November is the date which is traditionally given as the day on which over a thousand years of monastic history abruptly came to an end, Glastonbury Abbey as a corporate entity was already extinct before the judicial execution. The *Opus Dei* had ceased and the monastery was empty - its monks had been forcibly evicted, its servants dismissed and its goods seized – although no official instrument of surrender had been signed.

There is an addendum to our story. After Henry VIII's death in 1547, the rapacious monarch was succeeded by his weakly nine-year-old son Edward VI, whose regents were committed to the cause of Protestant reform. But on the accession of Edward's sister Mary Tudor in 1553, Catholicism was reintroduced. The new queen also encouraged a return to the religious life, by refounding a small number of monasteries, the most important of which was that associated with the royal abbey of Westminster. Four members of Westminster's new community had formerly been monks at Glastonbury and they had not forgotten their old home. In 1554 they petitioned the Lord Chamberlain for the restoration of Glastonbury Abbey to the Benedictine order, on the grounds of its 'being a house of such antiquity, and of fame through all Christendome, first begun by St Joseph of Arimathea, (who took down the dead body of our Saviour Christ from the Cross,) and lyeth buried in Glassenbury'.[110] But despite the best of intentions, the scheme was still-born and with the accession of Elizabeth I in 1558 and the suppression of Mary's fledgling houses the following year, any last hope of re-establishing Glastonbury was dashed.[111] Over eight hundred years of continuous worship, history and tradition had been finally and irretrievably brought to an end. There would be no further additions to the story of Glastonbury's sacred origins until a century had passed. When they did re-emerge into the light of day, it was into a world which had changed beyond all recognition.

Epilogue

The Reformation marked an important sea-change for the evolving narrative of Glastonbury's sacred origins. Before the Dissolution this story had been an in-house corporate tradition, controlled for the most part by a celibate Catholic community, and it demonstrates in microcosm the extraordinary fluidity and fusion of the literal, symbolic and metaphorical which was the dominant mode of late medieval Catholicism. After the Dissolution the tradition fragmented; now utilised by an array of Protestant and Catholic propagandists, the origin story re-emerged from the abbey's literary detritus and continued to evolve, incorporating both local folklore and the unfettered imagination. Thus storytelling about Glastonbury's origins came to play a minor but significant role in England's new Protestant foundation myth and its evolution continues to the present day.[112]

In its fundamentals, Glastonbury's medieval origin story remained remarkably consistent throughout the abbey's existence. The themes articulated by 'B' in the tenth century were, in their essentials, the same as those articulated by the anonymous author of the *Lyfe* of St Joseph half a millennium later. Glastonbury was chosen by God, dedicated to His Mother and had been established by the first British Christians. In this respect, it is the first theme, that Glastonbury was chosen by

Epilogue

God - set apart as a special place – which still has the greatest resonance with visitors today. Although long disconnected from its medieval origins, this notion of Glastonbury's 'otherness' can be found in most relevant modern literature, whether scholarly or popular, and expressed in one way or another in the numerous courses, conferences and workshops for which the town is famous. While many other English religious houses claimed divine sanction for their origins, Glastonbury alone claimed such an intimate association with the Godhead.

The story's second theme, Glastonbury's dedication by Christ to His Mother, is perhaps now the least well known – despite the official restoration of St Mary's shrine in the town's Roman Catholic church in 1955.[113] Ubiquitous in the sources we have considered, it is difficult to overemphasise the Virgin's significance to medieval Glastonbury. The very existence of the ancient Church of St Mary and the 'true' image of the Virgin it housed (and associated miraculous phenomena), demonstrated Glastonbury's pre-eminence as a Marian shrine. While medieval England had many other Marian shrines, not least Walsingham in Norfolk, only Glastonbury claimed a direct biblical connection to Christ's Mother through St Joseph of Arimathea. It is hardly surprising therefore that, when the Reformation's protagonists sought to advance their vision of a pure, early British church by removing perceived abuses of its medieval predecessor, the Virgin's pivotal role at Glastonbury was expunged from new variants of the foundation story and her former sanctuary fell into obscurity.

It is our story's third element, Glastonbury's foundation by the first British Christians, which attracted the only significant addition to our tale – the backdating of the Old Church's foundation to the period 'immediately after Christ's passion' and naming St Joseph of Arimathea as its founder.[114] This medieval 'St Joseph of Glastonbury' was a complex character, an exemplum, a holy helper and an intercessor who stood before the heavenly throne at the head of the long line of saints who made Glastonbury blessed. That St Joseph was incorporated into the abbey's origin narrative in the thirteenth century is unsurprising. The simple acknowledgement that Glastonbury was an ancient foundation 'B' had made at the end of the tenth century, and the speculations which William of Malmesbury had made in the early twelfth century were no longer enough; a prestigious founder was required. A necessary expedient based on the priorities of the medieval church, the abbey had suffered a devastating fire and the attentions of a predatory bishop; Glastonbury needed to exert its independence and the very best way to do this was by naming an illustrious founder. Ancient origins mattered, for antiquity granted authority and precedence in the medieval world, an element of ecclesiastical realpolitik of which Glastonbury took full advantage. This was particularly the case in the early fifteenth century when the abbey's origin was used to establish national precedence during the Conciliar movement.

But St Joseph's importance to late medieval England or Glastonbury should not be overstated. As Michael Protheroe has suggested, 'Glastonbury's Joseph legend was irrelevant to the polity of Christendom, beyond the jockeying for precedence during the Conciliar era, which only lasted a mere quarter of a century. Indeed its relative insignificance explains why it is passed over in silence in standard histories of the period.'[115]

Epilogue

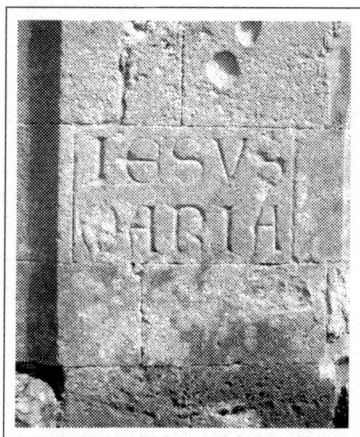

Fig. 11. The IESVS: MARIA stone,
situated on the south exterior wall
of the Lady Chapel.

While enthusiastically promoted as the Glastonbury's founder, St Joseph did not displace the Virgin as the abbey's patron and his image did not appear on the convent's seal. While pilgrimage to his subterranean chapel was encouraged, and miracles were attributed to his intercession, he was portrayed as subservient to the Virgin (appropriately his chapel was literally beneath hers) and he pointed the way to the mystery she embodied. As I have elsewhere observed, 'without the antiquity of St Mary's cult and the mystery surrounding its origins and the identity of its founder, St Joseph's adoption as the monastery's putative founder would have been impossible. Our Lady's cultus was the devotional focus around which Glastonbury Abbey grew in the centuries following the great fire of 1184 and it was the fundamental matrix in which the monastery's legendary foundation could take root.'[116]

Glastonbury: Origins of the Sacred

Ultimately, as the medieval sources demonstrate, it was not just Joseph as founder which was important, but his role as messenger, for he had brought the Christian faith to these shores, established the first British church and introduced devotion to Christ's Mother, Mary. Remarkably, the epitome of this message can still be found in the abbey ruins today, carved into the south exterior wall of the Lady Chapel, probably at some time in the thirteenth or fourteenth centuries. Variously described as a 'pilgrim station' or 'foundation stone', it may equally commemorate a significant moment in the abbey's history. Reading simply IESVS: MARIA (JESUS: MARY), the inscription can be eloquently expanded to read 'He made His home in her: She made her home in Him'. Thus the central message of the Incarnation of Christ through his mother Mary and the Salvation of all humankind through Christ is proclaimed in its simplest form. This is the fundamental truth which lies at the core of medieval Glastonbury's foundation story, for without this message there would have been no messenger and without the messenger there would be no Glastonbury.

But as our story's evolution demonstrates, Glastonbury's fame sprang from more than just its foundation narrative. Glastonbury was great, not just because of its patron St Mary or its founder St Joseph, but because of its continuing role as a centre of Christian culture, education and mission. The medieval pilgrim to Glastonbury saw evidence not only of its foundation, but also of its continual role as both 'mother' and 'tomb' of saints. Housing the shrines of such pivotal figures in British history as St Patrick of Ireland, St David of Wales and St Dunstan of Canterbury, and the relics of literally hundreds of other saints including apostles, popes and early martyrs, Glastonbury was a microcosm of Christendom – an earthly mirror of the New Jerusalem as John of Glastonbury dubbed it.[117] Administered by the Benedictine order, the abbey was not just the custodian of an extraordinary past, but a living, vibrant reality. While the Reformation produced its detractors, even Thomas Cromwell's notorious agent Richard Layton noted on his first visit to Glastonbury in 1535, that 'the brethren be so straight that they cannot offend', a judgement few other monasteries shared.[118]

But as Geoffrey Ashe has observed, there has been a regrettable tendency in recent years for alternative historians to push Glastonbury's origins back to an idealised pagan past and in so doing they largely ignore the Catholic Christian foundation story, upon which Glastonbury's myths and traditions so firmly stand.[119] This is unfortunate, for it diminishes our understanding of both the past and the present. As Joseph Armitage Robinson, Glastonbury's first modern scholar, wrote of the abbey's legends in 1926: 'He who rejects them as unworthy trivialities, and will have nothing but the unclothed skeleton of historically attested fact, cuts out the poetry from life, and renders himself incapable of understanding the fullness of his inheritance.'[120] It is particularly ironic, therefore, that in an age of religious pluralism and cultural diversity, that the richest and most fundamental element in Glastonbury's story has been largely rejected, replaced instead by modern imaginings which deny their own antecedents.

Finally and perhaps most remarkably of all, we should observe our story's longevity. By defining, explaining and laying claim to the past, the monks of Glastonbury sought to secure their present and guarantee an uncertain future. However, none of them could have foreseen the Reformation or guessed at its consequences for their abbey. But despite the breaking of the bonds of Catholic universalism in the sixteenth century, the story of Glastonbury's sacred origins endured. Creatively reinvented and embellished over the following centuries, modern Glastonbury attracts large numbers of people from spiritually and culturally diverse backgrounds, for whom the myths and legends of St Joseph of Arimathea, King Arthur and the first British church still make it a special place. In this respect the medieval story of Glastonbury's sacred origins was so successful that its effects are still being felt today, almost five hundred years after the institution that created 'Glastonbury' ceased to exist.

Notes

1   Carley, James (ed.) *The Chronicle of Glastonbury Abbey: An Edition, Translation and Study of John of Glastonbury's Cronica sive Antiquitates Glastoniensis Ecclesie* (Woodbridge: The Boydell Press, 1985) 176-177.

2   Carley *Chronicle* 30-33.

3   Cook, G.H. *Letters to Cromwell and Others on the Suppression of the Monasteries* (London: John Baker, 1965) 242.

4   This wall was constructed by Abbot Nicholas Frome (1420-1456). See Luxford, Julian *The Art and Architecture of English Benedictine Monasteries, 1300-1540: A Patronage History* (Woodbridge: The Boydell Press, 2005) 142.

5   For an inventory of the conventual buildings drawn up at the Suppression, see Collinson, John *The History and Antiquities of the County of Somerset* Vol. II (Bath: R. Cruttwell, 1791) 260-261. The original from which Collinson drew seemingly does not survive.

6   Watkin, Aelred *The Glastonbury Chartulary: Vol. I* (Frome: Somerset Record Society, 1947) Vol. lix, lvi.

7   Skeat, Walter W. (ed.) *Joseph of Arimathie Otherwise Called the Romance of the Seint Graal or Holy Grail* (London: Early English Text Society, 1871) 48.

8   For Glastonbury's early charters see Abrams, Lesley *Anglo-Saxon Glastonbury: Church and Endowment* (Woodbridge: The Boydell Press, 1996).

9   Abrams *Anglo-Saxon Glastonbury* 5.

10   Abrams *Anglo-Saxon Glastonbury* 27.

11   For a discussion of St Patrick at Glastonbury and his role in its evolving traditions, see Abrams, Lesley 'St Patrick and Glastonbury Abbey: Nihil Ex Nihilo Fit?' in Dumville, David N. (ed.) *Saint Patrick* (Woodbridge: The Boydell Press, 1993) 233-242.

12   For further discussion regarding the 'Old Church', see Protheroe, Michael J. 'New Light on the Mystery of Glastonbury's Old Church' in *Notes & Queries for Somerset and Dorset* Vol. XXXVI, September 2010, Part 372.

13   Winterbottom, M. & Lapidge, M. (ed. & trans.) *The Early Lives of St. Dunstan* (Oxford: Clarendon Press, 2012).

14   Winterbottom & Lapidge *The Early Lives* 12-13.

15   Winterbottom & Lapidge *The Early Lives* 12-13.

16   Ashdown, Paul *The Lord was at Glastonbury: Somerset and the Jesus Voyage Story* (Glastonbury: The Squeeze Press, 2010) 215-216.

17   Ashe, G. *King Arthur's Avalon: The Story of Glastonbury* (1957) (Stroud: Sutton Publishing, 2007) 31.

18   In 1081 Norman disregard for Anglo-Saxon customs culminated in bloodshed at Glastonbury. See Scott, John *The Early History of Glastonbury: An Edition, Translation and Study of William of Malmesbury's De Antiquitate Glastonie Ecclesie* (Woodbridge: The Boydell Press, 1981), 158-159.

19   Mynors, R.A.B., Thomson, R.M. & Winterbottom, M. (ed. & trans.) *Gesta Regnum Anglorum: The History of the English Kings* (2 Vols.) (Oxford: Clarendon Press, 1998) 810-811.

20   Although William's life of St Dunstan survives, sadly his lives of SS Patrick, Benignus and Indract exist now only as fragments. See Winterbottom, M. & Thomson, R.M. (ed. & trans) *William of Malmesbury: Saints' Lives* (Oxford: Oxford University Press, 2002).

21   For Bede's account of Eleutherius' mission to Lucius, see Colgrave, B. & Mynors, R.A.B. Bede's *Ecclesiastical History of the English People* (Oxford: Clarendon Press, 1969) 24-25 & 562-563.

22   Davis, R. *The Book of Pontiffs* (*Liber Pontificalis*) (Liverpool: Liverpool University Press, 2009) 6.

23   Mynors, Thomson, & Winterbottom *Gesta Regnum* 802-803.

24   Mynors, Thomson & Winterbottom *Gesta Regnum* 802-803.

25   Mynors, Thomson & Winterbottom *Gesta Regnum* 810-811.

26   James, J.W. *Rhigyfarch's Life of St. David: The Basic Mid Twelfth-century Latin Text with Introduction, Critical Apparatus and Translation* (Cardiff: University of Wales Press, 1967).

27   James Rhigyfarch's *Life of St. David* 1967 'For he founded in all twelve monasteries. First he reached Glastonbury, and built a church; next Bath, and here, rendering the death-dealing water health-giving by blessing it, he endowed it with a never-failing heat, making it suitable for the bathing of bodies.' 8 & 33.

28   On the altar of St David, see Scott *Early History* 80-83.

29   Scott *Early History* 66-67.

30   Gransden, Antonia 'The Growth of the Glastonbury Traditions and Legends in the Twelfth Century' in Gransden, Antonia *Legends, Traditions and History in Medieval England* (London: The Hambledon Press, 1992) 165.

31   Scott *Early History* 26.

32   Carley *Chronicle* 178-179.

33   Scott *Early History* 80-81.

34   Carley *Chronicle* 44-45.

35   There is no English translation of Adam of Domerham's chronicle. See Standen, David Charles '*Libellus de rebus gestis Glastoniensibus*', *Attributed to Adam of Damerham, a Monk of Glastonbury, Edited with Introduction and Critical Notes* (University of London, 2000) Unpublished PhD thesis.

36   Carley *Chronicle* 174-175.

37   This reference to Blois' abbacy as in the past enables us to establish that this chapter is not William's work, since Blois did not die until 1171, long after William had completed his chronicle.

38   Scott *Early History* 50-51.

39   St Denis was a third-century Bishop of Paris, martyred in the Decian persecution shortly after 250 AD. He was conflated with two other people of the same name. One was the first-century Greek pagan convert whom the apostle Paul persuaded of the Christian faith on the Areopagus in Athens (Acts 17: 34). The second was the fifth- or sixth-century Syrian, now known as the Pseudo-Dionysius, who claimed in his Greek language mystical works to be the Pauline convert to give his works quasi-apostolic authority.

40   See Lagorio, Valerie M. 'The Evolving Legend of St. Joseph of Glastonbury'
        in *Speculum: A Journal of Medieval Studies* Vol. XLVI, No. 2, April 1971, 218
        and Protheroe, Michael J. 'Glastonbury as Roma Secunda: An Excursus' in
        Notes & Queries for Somerset and Dorset Vol. XXXVII, September 2011, Part
        374.

41   For example, William includes the text of a 'privilege' dated 965, granted by
        Pope John XII, which had been 'humbly besought by Edgar, glorious king
        of the English, and Dunstan, Archbishop of the holy church of Canterbury'
        by which 'the monastery of St. Mary of Glastonbury' was received 'into the
        bosom of the Roman church and the protection of the blessed apostles'. See
        Scott *Early History* 128-129.

42   For a concise overview of Arthur's association with Glastonbury Abbey,
        see James P. Carley's 'Arthur in English History' in Barron, W.R.J. (ed.)
        *The Arthur of the English: The Arthurian Legend in Medieval English Life and
        Literature* (Cardiff: University of Wales Press, 2001) 47-57.

43   For a detailed consideration of Arthur's tomb, see Lindley, Philip *Tomb
        Destruction and Scholarship: Medieval Monuments in Early Modern England*
        (Donington: Shaun Tyas, 2007) 138-166.

44   Watkin *The Glastonbury Chartulary: Vol. I*, xlix & 110.

45   Griscom, A. *Historia Regum Britanniae of Geoffrey of Monmouth* (London:
        Longmans, Green & Co., 1929) 438.

46   Carley *Chronicle* 24-25 & 78-79.

47   See Mark 15: 43.

48   In the Middle Ages the founders of national churches were usually accorded
        'apostolic' status. See Hayward, Paul 'Gregory the Great as "Apostle of the
        English" in Post-Conquest Canterbury' in *Journal of Ecclesiastical History* Vol.
        55, No. I, January 2004, 22-31.

49   Carley *Chronicle* 192-193.

50   We should note that although the legal process to change Glastonbury's
        status from abbey to cathedral-priory was initiated it quickly stalled. Thus
        the monastery existed in a legal limbo for a number of years, neither wholly
        abbey nor wholly cathedral, but fulfilling the functions of both.

51   The diocese of Wells was created in 909, before being moved to Bath in
        1090 when Wells lost cathedral status. After the failure of Savaric's diocese
        of Bath and Glastonbury, Wells regained its status in 1245 when it was
        united with Bath to form the diocese of Bath and Wells.

Notes

52   The goal of pilgrimage for almost three hundred years, the 'holy cross of Bromeholme' immortalised by Chaucer in his 'Reeve's Tale' ultimately disappeared in the dark days of the Reformation. For the Cross of Bromholm see Wormald, Francis 'The Rood of Bromholm' in *Journal of the Warburg Institute* Vol. I, No. 1 July 1937, 31-45.

53   Carley *Chronicle* 202-203.

54   Carley *Chronicle* 30-31.

55   Although the *Carta sancti Patricii* is traditionally dated to *circa* 1220, the incorporation of material in the text which subordinates Wells to Glastonbury suggests a composition date closer to 1245 when Wells officially became the seat of the bishop.

56   Scott *Early History* 56-57.

57   Scott *Early History* 56-57. It is interesting to speculate if the three crowns incorporated into Glastonbury's shield of arms in the early sixteenth century represent the three pagan kings who gave land to the first Christian missionaries recorded in the *Carta sancti Patricii*.

58   Carley *Chronicle* 96-99.

59   Carley *Chronicle* 100-101.

60   Scott *Early History* 44-45.

61   A later marginal note appended to chapter 2 of the *De Antiquitate* also refers to Joseph's role in various secular Arthurian romances. It should be noted that the verse *Joseph d'Arimathie* of Robert de Boron had already pictured Joseph sending the company of the grail west to the 'vales of Avaron', *vaus de Avaron*, which is generally identified with Glastonbury/Avalon.

62   Scott *Early History* 44-45.

63   For a consideration of miraculous foundation stories and the contexts which created them, see Scott *Early History* 27-33.

64   Scott *Early History* 48-49.

65   Carley *Chronicle* 44-45.

66   Stourton was active in the first quarter of the fourteenth century. He is also known to have written *De Laude beate Virginis* which survives at Oxford (Oxford, Bodleian MS Bodl. 159).

67   For the full text of the agreement made on February 22nd 1333, see Watkin *Great Chartulary: Vol. 3*, ccxliii-ccxliv.

68   See Smith, Lucy Toulmin *The Itinerary of John Leland,* London: George Bell and Sons, 1907, *Vol. 1*, 1907, 289.

69   Watkin, Aelred 'Glastonbury, 1538-9, as shown by its Account Rolls' in
        Downside Review Vol. 67, No. 209, July 1949, 443, 445, 448 & 449.

70   Although James Carley identified John of Glastonbury with John Seen
        and his hypothesis has been generally accepted, not all scholars agree. See
        Gransden, Antonia 'The Date and Authorship of John of Glastonbury's
        Cronica sive Antiquitates Glastoniensis Ecclesie' in Gransden, Antonia *Leg-
        ends, Traditions and History in Medieval England* (London: The Hambledon
        Press, 1992) 289-298.

71   For a detailed consideration of John of Glastonbury's *Cronica* and the
        context in which it was created, see Carley *Chronicle* xi-xlv.

72   Carley *Chronicle* xxx.

73   Carley *Chronicle* 4-5.

74   Carley *Chronicle* 128-131.

75   Carley *Chronicle* 8-9.

76   Carley *Chronicle* 10-11.

77   Watkins *The Glastonbury Chartulary: Vol. I*, xvi.

78   Carley *Chronicle* 28-29 and Scott *Early History* 82-83.

79   Carley *Chronicle* 32-33.

80   Carley *Chronicle* 50-51.

81   Carley *Chronicle* 52-53.

83   For a detailed consideration of Melkin's Prophesy, see: Carley, James
        'Melkin the Bard and Esoteric Tradition at Glastonbury Abbey' in *Downside
        Review* Vol. 99, 1981, 1-17 & Carley *Chronicle* (1985) xlviii-lx.

84   Carley *Arthur in English History* 52.

85   Carley *Chronicle* 12-13.

86   For the complete text, see Robinson, Joseph A. *Two Glastonbury Legends*
        (Cambridge: Cambridge University Press, 1926) 63-64.

87   For St Joseph's relics, see Thomas, Islwyn G. *The Cult of Saints' Relics in Me-
        dieval England* (University of London, 1974) Unpublished PhD thesis, 418.

88   For the *Magna Tabula* see Krochalis, Jeanne 'Magna Tabula: The Glas-
        tonbury Tablets (Parts 1 and 2)' in Carley, James *Glastonbury Abbey and the
        Arthurian Tradition* (Woodbridge: D.S. Brewer, 2001) 435-567.

89   For a consideration of the brass plate and the text it bore in Latin and
        English translation, see Goodall, John A. 'The Glastonbury Abbey Memorial
        Plate Reconsidered' in *The Antiquaries Journal* Vol. LXVI, 1986, 364-368.

Notes

90   Goodall 'The Glastonbury Abbey Memorial Plate' 366.

91   For the complete English text of Thomas Poulton's protest delivered at
      Constance, see Crowder, C.M.D. *Unity, Heresy and Reform 1378-1460:
      The Conciliar Response to the Great Schism* (London: Edward Arnold, 1977)
      110-126.

92   Crowder *Unity, Heresy and Reform* 119.

93   Lagorio 'The Evolving Legend', 223.

94   Lagorio 'The Evolving Legend', 223, fn. 64.

95   Carley *Culture* 140.

96   The images of St Joseph of Arimathea which appear on the rood screen in
      Plymtree Parish Church in Devon and in stained glass in the east window
      in Langport Parish Church in Somerset were almost certainly influenced by
      the saint's promotion at Glastonbury.

97   Brown, Michelle P. *The Holkham Bible Picture Book: A Facsimile* (London:
      The British Library, 2007) 78 & f.33.

98   Rigg, A.G. *A Glastonbury Miscellany of the Fifteenth Century* (Oxford: Ox-
      ford University Press, 1968) 120-122.

99   Smith, *The Itinerary,* 288.

100   For Richard Beere's career, see Radford, C.A.R. *Abbot Richard Beere (1493-
      1524)* (unpublished report) National Monuments Record Swindon, NMR
      GLA PUB/13, 10-29.

101   Skeat *Joseph of Arimathie* 37-52.

102   Skeat *Joseph of Arimathie* 43.

103   From the Greek αχεροποίητα 'not handmade'.

104   The most renowned of these images in the medieval west was the achei-
      ropoietos icon of Christ in the papal oratory of the Sancta Sanctorum in
      Rome, which was believed to have been begun by St Luke and finished by
      angels. See Kirstin, Noreen 'Revealing the Sacred: The Icon of Christ in
      the Sancta Sanctorum, Rome' in *Word & Image* (London: Taylor & Francis,
      2006) Vol. 22, No. 3, 2006, 228-237.

105   Admittedly, the circumstances surrounding the supposed origins of almost
      all English 'miraculous' cult images are lost to us, but Glastonbury's claim
      would still appear exceptional.

106   After the Great Fire of 1184, the new building which replaced the *Vetusta
      Ecclesia* was known concurrently as the 'Old Church', the 'Church of St.
      Mary' and the 'Lady Chapel'. This fluid nomenclature, clearly expressing its
      multiple roles, persisted until the Dissolution in 1539.

107 The Benedictine scholar Dom Aelred Watkin suggested that the chief Marian feast observed at Glastonbury was Our Lady's Nativity (8 September) seemingly based on the evidence of an eleventh-century charter which states that 'on the feast of Our Lady's Nativity people come to the monastery to pray' and that the earliest fair granted to the abbey by Henry I, *circa* 1131, commenced on the Nativity of the Blessed Virgin. The dedication of the chapel to the Assumption in the anonymous verse *Lyfe* would suggest that the Assumption had replaced the Nativity as Glastonbury's primary Marian feast by the sixteenth century. See Watkin, Aelred *The Story of Glastonbury Abbey* (London: The Catholic Truth Society, 1960) 15 & Watkin, Aelred (ed.) *The Glastonbury Chartulary: Vol. 1* (SRS) Vol. 59, 1944, liv & lxvii-lxviii.

108 Skeat *Joseph of Arimathie* 48.

109 Skeat *Joseph of Arimathie* 51.

110 See Warner, Richard *An History of the Abbey of Glaston: And of the Town of Glastonbury* (Bath: Cruttwell, 1826) Appendix xlv.

111 For a recent assessment of the attempted restoration of Glastonbury under Mary, see: Knighton, C.S. 'Westminster Abbey Restored' in Duffy, E. & Loades, D. (eds.) *The Church of Mary Tudor* (Aldershot: Ashgate Publishing, 2006) 84-85.

112 For a brief introduction to the post-Reformation development of the foundation story, see Walsham, Alexandra *The Reformation of the Landscape: Religion, Identity, and Memory in Early Modern Britain and Ireland* (Oxford: Oxford University Press, 2011) 492-497.

113 See Protheroe, Michael J. 'Towards a Catholic Historiography of Post-Dissolution Glastonbury in *Downside Review* Vol. 130, No. 458, January 2012, 53-78.

114 By the late Middle Ages, it was generally agreed that Glastonbury had been founded in the year 63 although at the Council of Constance the English delegation pushed the date even further back, claiming the Joseph had journeyed to England 'immediately after Christ's passion'. See Crowder *Unity, Heresy and Reform* 119.

115 Protheroe, Michael *Glastonbury, Joseph of Arimathea, and Rome* (unpublished).

116 See Hopkinson-Ball, Timothy 'The Cultus of Our Lady at Glastonbury Abbey: 1184-1539' in *Downside Review* Vol. 130, No. 458, January 2012, 3-52.

Notes

117   See Carley, James and Howley, Martin 'Relics at Glastonbury in the Fourteenth Century: An Annotated Edition of British Library, Cotton Titus D.vii, fols. 2r-13v¹' in Carley, *Glastonbury Abbey and the Arthurian Tradition* 569-616.

118   See Cook *Letters to Cromwell* 40.

119   See Ashe *King Arthur's Avalon* xvi.

120   Robinson *Two Glastonbury Legends* 50.

Bibliography

Abrams, Lesley 'St Patrick and Glastonbury Abbey:
Nihil Ex Nihilo Fit?' in Dumville, David N. (ed.) *Saint Patrick*
(Woodbridge: The Boydell Press, 1993).

Abrams, Lesley *Anglo-Saxon Glastonbury: Church and
Endowment* (Woodbridge: The Boydell Press, 1996).

Ashdown, Paul *The Lord was at Glastonbury: Somerset and the
Jesus Voyage Story* (Glastonbury: The Squeeze Press, 2010).

Ashe, G. *King Arthur's Avalon: The Story of Glastonbury* (1957)
(Stroud: Sutton Publishing, 2007).

Brown, Michelle P. *The Holkham Bible Picture Book:
A Facsimile* (London: The British Library, 2007).

Carley, James 'Melkin the Bard and Esoteric Tradition at
Glastonbury Abbey' in *Downside Review* Vol. 99, 1981.

Carley, James (ed.) *The Chronicle of Glastonbury Abbey:
An Edition, Translation and Study of John of Glastonbury's Cronica
sive Antiquitates Glastoniensis Ecclesie* (Woodbridge: The Boydell
Press, 1985).

Carley, James 'Arthur in English History' in Barron, W.R.J.
(ed.) *The Arthur of the English: The Arthurian Legend in Medieval
English Life and Literature* (Cardiff: University of Wales Press,
2001).

Carley, James and Howley, Martin 'Relics at Glastonbury
in the Fourteenth Century: An Annotated Edition of British

Bibliography

Library, Cotton Titus D.vii, fols. 2r-13v[1]' in Carley, James *Glastonbury Abbey and the Arthurian Tradition* (Woodbridge: D.S. Brewer, 2001).

Colgrave, B. & Mynors, R.A.B. *Bede's Ecclesiastical History of the English People* (Oxford: Clarendon Press, 1969).

Collinson, John *The History and Antiquities of the County of Somerset* Vol. II (Bath: R. Cruttwell, 1791).

Cook, G.H. *Letters to Cromwell and Others on the Suppression of the Monasteries* (London: John Baker, 1965).

Crowder, C.M.D. *Unity, Heresy and Reform 1378-1460: The Conciliar Response to the Great Schism* (London: Edward Arnold, 1977).

Davis, R. *The Book of Pontiffs (Liber Pontificalis)* (Liverpool: Liverpool University Press, 2009).

Goodall, John A. 'The Glastonbury Abbey Memorial Plate Reconsidered' in *The Antiquaries Journal* Vol. LXVI, 1986.

Gransden, Antonia 'The Date and Authorship of John of Glastonbury's Cronica sive Antiquitates Glastoniensis Ecclesie' in Gransden, Antonia *Legends, Traditions and History in Medieval England* (London: The Hambledon Press, 1992).

Gransden, Antonia 'The Growth of the Glastonbury Traditions and Legends in the Twelfth Century' in Gransden, Antonia *Legends, Traditions and History in Medieval England* (London: The Hambledon Press, 1992).

Griscom, A. *Historia Regum Britanniae of Geoffrey of Monmouth* (London: Longmans, Green & Co., 1929).

Hayward, Paul 'Gregory the Great as 'Apostle of the English' in Post-Conquest Canterbury' in *Journal of Ecclesiastical History* Vol. 55, No. I, January 2004.

Hopkinson-Ball, Timothy 'The Cultus of Our Lady at Glastonbury Abbey: 1184-1539' in *Downside Review* Vol. 130, No. 458, January 2012.

James, J.W. *Rhigyfarch's Life of St. David: The Basic Mid Twelfth-century Latin Text with Introduction, Critical Apparatus and Translation* (Cardiff: University of Wales Press, 1967).

Kirstin, Noreen 'Revealing the Sacred: The Icon of Christ in the Sancta Sanctorum, Rome' in *Word & Image* (London: Taylor & Francis, 2006) Vol. 22, No. 3, 2006.

Knighton, C.S. 'Westminster Abbey Restored' in Duffy, E. & Loades, D. (eds.) *The Church of Mary Tudor* (Aldershot: Ashgate Publishing, 2006).

Krochalis, Jeanne 'Magna Tabula: The Glastonbury Tablets (Parts 1 and 2)' in Carley, James *Glastonbury Abbey and the Arthurian Tradition* (Woodbridge: D.S. Brewer, 2001).

Lagorio, Valerie M. 'The Evolving Legend of St. Joseph of Glastonbury' in *Speculum: A Journal of Medieval Studies* Vol. XLVI, No. 2, April 1971

Lindley, Philip *Tomb Destruction and Scholarship: Medieval Monuments in Early Modern England* (Donington: Shaun Tyas, 2007).

Luxford, Julian *The Art and Architecture of English Benedictine Monasteries, 1300-1540: A Patronage History* (Woodbridge: The Boydell Press, 2005).

Mynors, R.A.B., Thomson, R.M. & Winterbottom, M. (ed. & trans.) *Gesta Regnum Anglorum: The History of the English Kings* (2 Vols.) (Oxford: Clarendon Press, 1998).

Protheroe, Michael J. 'New Light on the Mystery of Glastonbury's Old Church' in *Notes & Queries for Somerset and Dorset* Vol. XXXVI, September 2010, Part 372.

Bibliography

Protheroe, Michael J. 'Glastonbury as Roma Secunda:
An Excursus' in *Notes & Queries for Somerset and Dorset* Vol.
XXXVII, September 2011, Part 374.

Protheroe, Michael J. 'Towards a Catholic Historiography
of Post-Dissolution Glastonbury in *Downside Review* Vol. 130,
No. 458, January 2012.

Protheroe, Michael *Glastonbury, Joseph of Arimathea, and Rome*
(unpublished).

Radford, C.A.R. *Abbot Richard Beere (1493-1524)*
(Unpublished report).

Rigg, A.G. *A Glastonbury Miscellany of the Fifteenth Century*
(Oxford: OUP, 1968).

Robinson, Joseph A. *Two Glastonbury Legends*
(Cambridge: CUP, 1926).

Scott, John *The Early History of Glastonbury: An Edition,
Translation and Study of William of Malmesbury's De Antiquitate
Glastonie Ecclesie* (Woodbridge: The Boydell Press, 1981).

Skeat, Walter W. (ed.) *Joseph of Arimathie Otherwise Called
the Romance of the Seint Graal Or Holy Grail* (London: Early
English Text Society, 1871).

Smith, Lucy Toulmin *The Itinerary of John Leland*
(London: George Bell and Sons, 1907).

Thomas, Islwyn G. *The Cult of Saints' Relics in Medieval England*
University of London, 1974) Unpublished PhD thesis.

Standen, David Charles *'Libellus de rebus gestis Glastoniensibus',
Attributed to Adam of Damerham, a Monk of Glastonbury, Edited
with Introduction and Critical Notes* (University of London,
2000) Unpublished PhD thesis.

Walsham, Alexandra *The Reformation of the Landscape: Religion,*

Identity, and Memory in Early Modern Britain and Ireland (Oxford: Oxford University Press, 2011).

Warner, Richard *An History of the Abbey of Glaston: And of the Town of Glastonbury* (Bath: Cruttwell, 1826).

Watkin, Aelred *The Glastonbury Chartulary: Vol. I* (Frome: Somerset Record Society, 1947) Vol. LIX.

Watkin, Aelred 'Glastonbury, 1538-9, as shown by its Account Rolls' in *Downside Review* Vol. 67, No. 209, July 1949.

Watkin, Aelred *The Story of Glastonbury Abbey* (London: The Catholic Truth Society, 1960).

Winterbottom, M. & Thomson, R.M. (ed. & trans) *William of Malmesbury: Saints' Lives* (Oxford: Oxford University Press, 2002).

Winterbottom, M. & Lapidge, M. (ed. & trans.) *The Early Lives of St. Dunstan* (Oxford: Clarendon Press, 2012).

Wormald, Francis 'The Rood of Bromholm' in *Journal of the Warburg Institute* Vol. I, No. 1 July 1937.

Map and Key

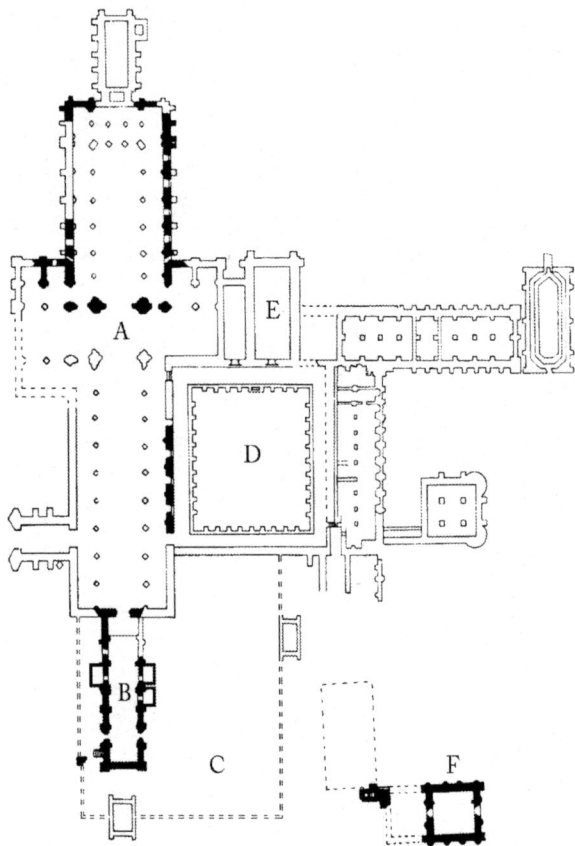

Fig. 12. Glastonbury Abbey
General plan, *circa* 1530

Glastonbury Abbey – Key

A. Abbey Church of SS Peter & Paul.

B. Church of St Mary / Lady Chapel.

C. Old Cemetery.

D. Cloister.

E. Chapter House.

F. Abbot's kitchen.

Solid Black – upstanding walls

Outline – foundations and conjectural

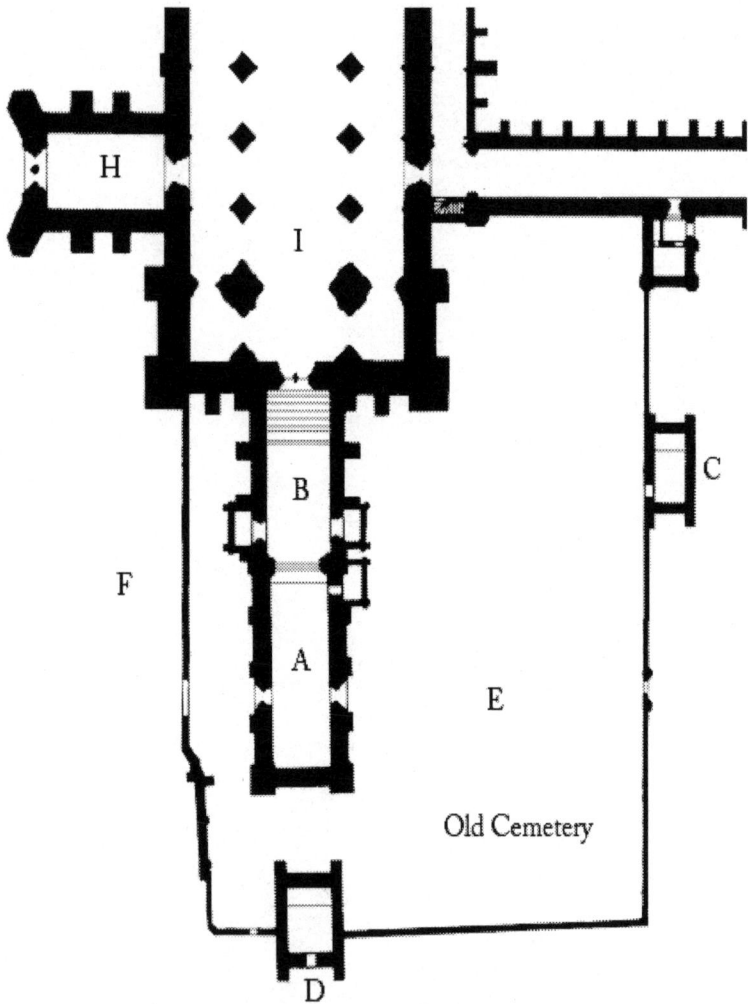

Fig. 13. Glastonbury Abbey
Conjectural plan of the Lady Chapel complex
at the west end of the nave, *circa* 1530.

Lady Chapel Complex – Key

A. Church of St Mary / Lady Chapel.

B. Lady Altar and 'miraculous' image of the Virgin.

C. Charnel Chapel of SS Michael & Joseph.

D. Chapel of St John the Baptist.

E. Approx. position of King Arthur's grave excavated in 1191.

F. Approx. position of St David's Pillar.

G. Stairs leading down to the crypt Chapel of St Joseph of Arimathea.

H. North Porch.

I. West end of nave.

Index

A

Abbadare 52
Abbey's official shield 31
Abbot Beere 70, 71
Abbot Chinnock 59, 60
Abrams, Lesley 9
Acheiropoietos 72, 89
Adam of Domerham 25, 85
Adam of Sodbury 45
Aethelwold 49
Alban, St 55
Aldhelm, St 9
Anglo-Saxon 9, 12, 17, 83, 84, 92
Anglo-Saxon Chronicle 9
Anselm, St 14
Apollinaris, St 14
Apollo 5
Apostolic Library 64
Archaeology 3, 4
Archbishop 14, 86
Architect of Heaven 44
Arthur, King 6, 2, 29, 30, 31, 32, 69, 82, 84, 86, 88, 91, 92, 101
Ashe, Geoffrey 11, 81, 84, 91, 92
Assumption of the Virgin 51, 73, 90
Avignon 62

B

Baldred 9
Barnabas, St 35, 73
Basel 62
Basilica 35, 63
Bath 5, 18, 23, 33, 34, 50, 63, 64, 83, 85, 86, 90, 93, 96

Beckery 31
Bede, St 15, 84, 93
Beere, Richard 70, 89, 95
Benignus, St 70, 84
Bishop Hallum of Salisbury 62
Bishop's Palace 74
Black marble sarcophagus 30
Blaise, St 36
Blome, John 56
Bodleian Library 58
Bradford upon Avon 3
Brass plate 61, 88
Bromholm Priory 35
'B', (Vita's author) 10, 12, 16, 76, 78
Byzantine Emperors 35
Byzantine Empire 34

C

Caduceus 70
Canonical Hours 47
Canterbury 14, 27, 55, 58, 80, 86, 93
Caradoc of Llancarvan 30
Carley, James 32, 49, 52, 53, 83, 85, 86, 87, 88, 89, 91, 92, 93, 94
Carta Henrici regis secundi 25
Carta sancti Patricii episcopi 37
Cathedrals 58
Caxton 68, 69
Celestine III, Pope 33
Celtic 22
Chantry 70
Charnel chapel 59, 60, 66
Charter of St Patrick 37
Charters 2, 6, 7, 9, 27, 28, 83
Chinnock, John 58, 59, 60
Christ 11, 12, 16, 17, 18, 21, 27, 31,

Index

37, 39, 40, 42, 43, 44, 50, 51,
53, 54, 55, 56, 59, 61, 63, 64,
68, 70, 71, 73, 75, 77, 78, 80,
89, 90, 94
Christchurch 58
Christianity 16, 36, 37, 49, 64, 71
Christopher the martyr 36
Chronica Majora 67
Chronicle 15, 22, 23, 48, 49, 51, 85
Church of St Mary 9, 13, 23, 25,
77, 99
City of Zara 35
Clerks of Our Lady 47, 70
Coel, King 36
Colchester 36
Communion of Saints 21
Compostela 38
Comyn, Eustace 35
Conciliar movement 62
Constance 62, 63, 89, 90
Constantine the Great, Emperor
36, 63
Constantinople 34, 35, 36, 58
Corbels 70
Council at Pisa 62
Cronica sive Antiquitates
Glastoniensis Ecclesie 48,
83, 88, 92, 93
Crucifixion 54, 68, 71
Crypt chapel 19, 70
Cuthbert, St 27

D
Dalmatia 35
David, St 6, 17, 18, 48, 52, 61, 73,
80, 83, 84, 85, 92, 94, 95,
101

De Antiquitate Glastonie Ecclesie 15,
95
Decurion 47 32
De nominibus Ihesu et Marie 45
Deruvian, St 38, 39, 44, 60, 66
De Sancto Joseph ab Armathia 69
Diocese 33, 34, 63, 64, 86
Dionysius the Areopagite, St 28
Dissolution 2, 2, 19, 47, 58, 67, 68,
70, 74, 76, 90, 95
Divine Office 47
Dream 17
Drops of blood 70
Dunstan, St 10, 14, 16, 49, 80, 84,
86, 96
Durham 27, 58

E
Edgar, King 13, 14, 86
Edmund Ironside, King 13
Edmund the Elder, King 13
Edward I, King 30
Edward III, King 50, 56
Edward VI, King 74
Eleutherius, Pope 15, 16, 38, 84
Elizabeth I, Queen 75
England 1, 2, 8, 13, 20, 27, 36, 45,
49, 50, 53, 55, 58, 62, 63, 64,
71, 73, 76, 77, 78, 85, 86, 88,
90, 93, 94, 95
Ephesians 51
Episcopal throne 41
Erasmus 70

F
Fitzgeldwin, Savaric 33
Fitzstephen, Ralph 23
Forests 54

103

Forged 6
Fourth Crusade 34
Fraudulent 30
Frome, Nicholas 64, 65, 83, 96

G
Gabriel, archangel 38, 43
Galahad grail quest 68
Geoffrey of Monmouth 31, 54, 86
George, St 36
Gesta Regum Anglorum 15
Gildas, St 21, 30
Glastonbury monk 26, 27, 45, 48,
        68, 71
Glastonbury Tor 39
Godfrey, monk of Glastonbury 27,
        28
Gold 20, 60
Golden ampoules 70
Gransden, Antonia 21
Great Chartulary 6, 87
Great Fire 5, 23
Great sapphire altar 18, 20
Guinevere, Queen 29, 30

H
Hardyng, John 68
Helen, St 36
Henry II, King 23, 25
Henry of Blois 13, 18, 27
Henry V, King 64, 66
Henry VIII, King 1, 74
Heorstan and Cynethryth 10
Heraclius, Patriarch of Rome 25
Historians 4, 29, 81
Holkham Bible 68, 89, 92
Holy Blood 53
Holy Grail 53, 83, 95

Holy Land 58, 71
Holy Sepulchre 70
Holy Spirit 44
Honorius, Pope III 34
House of Lords 1
Humanist 70

I
IESVS: MARIA 6, 79, 80
Incarnation 80
Indract 21, 84
Ine of Wessex, King 4, 9, 40
Inheritance 81
Ireland 80, 90, 96
Island of Apples 54
Isle of Avalon 29, 52

J
Jacob of Voragine's 67
James, St 32, 38, 49, 52, 83, 84, 85,
        86, 88, 91, 92, 93, 94
Jerusalem 20, 25, 35, 36, 54, 81
John of Glastonbury 1, 24, 48, 69,
        70, 71, 81, 83, 88, 92
John Seen 48, 88
John the Baptist, St 35, 101
John XXII, Pope 45, 50, 86
Josephat 53
Joseph de Marmore 53
Joseph of Arimathea, St 2, 6, 2, 32,
        42, 44, 49, 51, 52, 53, 56,
        57, 58, 61, 62, 63, 64, 65,
        69, 72, 75, 77, 78, 82, 89, 90,
        95, 101
Judas 41

K
Kent 14
Knotted cross 70

Index

L

Ladder of heaven 54
Lady Chapel 2, 6, 19, 23, 25, 29, 45, 47, 48, 49, 59, 60, 61, 69, 73, 79, 80, 90, 99, 101
Lawrence the martyr 36
Layton, Richard 81
Lead cross 29
Legend 2, 6, 7, 12, 51, 64, 71, 74, 78
Legenda Aurea 67
Leland, John 7, 70, 89, 95
Le Morte d'Arthur 68
Liber Pontificalis 15, 84, 93
Library 6, 7, 15
Life of St Gildas 30
Lignea basilica 9
Lions 30
London 25, 56, 71, 83, 85, 86, 88, 89, 90, 92, 93, 94, 95, 96
Loreto 70
Lost book 45
Lucius, King 5
Luke the evangelist 36

M

Magna Tabula 58, 61, 88, 94
Magnum priviligium regis Inae 40
Malmesbury 6, 14, 15, 22, 23, 24, 27, 37, 38, 40, 42, 48, 51, 52, 53, 78, 84, 95, 96
Malory, Thomas 68
Manuscripts 6, 7
Marian shrine 77
Mark's Gospel 32
Mark the evangelist 36
Martyr 14, 28, 36, 55
Mary Tudor, Queen 74, 90, 94

Mater Sanctorum 26
Matrix 79
Mediterranean world 34
Melkin 52, 54, 88, 92
Mercury 70, 71
Messenger 70, 71, 80
Michael the archangel 39
Miraculous 2, 11, 12, 25, 27, 45, 49, 60, 69, 72, 77, 87, 89, 101
Monasteries 1, 3, 18, 33, 35, 58, 74, 81, 85
Monastery 1, 2, 3, 13, 14, 18, 20, 22, 23, 24, 27, 28, 33, 35, 47, 48, 51, 56, 60, 67, 71, 74, 79, 86, 90
Monk 15, 18, 26, 27, 28, 45, 48, 68, 71
Mosaic 21
Mother of God 11, 24, 27, 47, 49, 51
Mother of Saints 26, 28
Muslim 35

N

Nazareth 68, 70
Nennius 31
Neophytes 11, 12, 16, 17
Norfolk 35, 77
Norman 5, 13, 14, 23, 27, 84

O

Office for the Dead 47
Old Cemetery 29, 36, 47, 59, 65, 69, 73, 99
Old Church 9, 13, 20, 21, 22, 23, 24, 27, 38, 39, 44, 49, 50, 53, 62, 78, 84, 90, 94
Oratory 11, 39, 52, 89

Orthodox 35

P
Pagan 38, 71, 81, 85, 87
Papal captivity 62
Paris 27, 67, 85
Patriarch 20, 25
Patrick, St 9, 37, 39, 80, 83, 92
Paul, St 28
Pavia-Siena 62
Peter of Spain 35
Peter, St 5, 63
Phagan, St 38, 39, 44, 59, 66
Philip, St 16, 17, 35, 36, 38, 40, 42, 51, 86, 94
Pilgrimage 1, 29, 38, 39, 71, 73, 79, 87
Pilgrims 23, 29, 59, 60, 69
Pillar of St David 61
Polton, Thomas 63
Porphyry 18
Portable altar 18
Privilege 6, 25, 28, 40, 41, 50, 86
Prophesy of Melkin 52
Protestant reform 74
Protheroe, Michael 78, 84, 86, 90, 94, 95
Purgatory 21
Pyramids 29

R
Ralph, Bishop of Bath 50
Reformation 76, 77, 81, 82, 87, 90, 95
Regents 74
Reginald, Bishop of Bath 23
Relics 4, 13, 14, 20, 21, 22, 26, 30, 34, 35, 36, 37, 41, 53, 58, 59, 60, 66, 72, 80, 88
Religion 1, 4, 5, 20, 21, 40, 49
Religious pluralism 81
Reliquaries 36
Renaissance man 70
Rhigyfarch 18, 84, 85, 94
Robinson, Joseph Armitage 81, 88, 91, 95
Rock-crystal cross 31
Roman deity 70
Roman Empire 63
Romanesque 13
Roma Secunda 28, 86, 95
Rome 16, 28, 33, 41, 50, 58, 62, 63, 64, 89, 90, 94, 95
Royal bones 29, 30

S
Sacraments 41
Sacred mystery 20, 21
Sanctity 6, 14, 20, 22, 28, 37, 49, 50, 58, 73
Saxon 3, 4, 9, 12, 13, 14, 17, 83, 84, 92
Schism 62, 63
Scholar 18, 52, 70, 81, 90
Scholastica, St 36
Scriptorium 42
Second Rome' 28, 50
Shield 31, 70, 87
Shrine 20, 27, 38, 72, 77
Silver 20, 35, 53
Somerset 3, 18, 57, 65, 83, 84, 86, 89, 92, 93, 94, 95, 96
Spheres of prophesy 52, 53
Square 21
Stained glass 67

Index

Statue 13, 24, 25, 27, 46, 47, 60, 69, 72, 73
St Denis 27, 28
Stephen the protomartyr 36
Stourton, Edmund 45
Swithun, St 27

T
Temple Church 25
Thomas, St 35
Tiled floor 21
Townsend, David 52
Tradition 15, 16, 18, 29, 42, 53, 75, 76
Triangle 21
Trinity College 68
Troteman, Joscelin 34
True Cross 35, 36, 63
Twelve portions of land 38
Twelve saints 43, 61
Tynemouth 58

V
Vellum sheets 58
Venice 35
Vetusta Ecclesia 9
Vincent of Saragossa, St 14
Virgin Mary 5, 10, 13, 24, 25, 26, 27, 31, 37, 38, 41, 43, 44, 45, 47, 48, 49, 51, 52, 54, 60, 68, 69, 72, 73, 77, 79, 90, 101
Vision 17, 43, 77
Vita Dauidis 18
Vita Dunstanae 10
Vita Gildae 30
Vita Merlini 54

W
Wales 17, 18, 80, 84, 86, 92, 94
Walnut 73
Walsingham 77
Weary-all Hill 73
Wellias 39
Wells 2, 3, 34, 39, 40, 41, 64, 74, 86, 87
Whiting, Richard 74
William of Malmesbury 6, 14, 22, 23, 24, 27, 37, 38, 40, 42, 48, 51, 52, 53, 78, 84, 95, 96
William Duke of Normandy 13,
Winchester 27
Wooden church 9, 61
Wooden statue 24
Worcester 63

Y
Yniswitrin 37
York 63